Izabela~

Love you spirit

Enjoy Bible study

and your kind soul

M Serena

# The White Picket Fence

## GOD'S TEST PILOT II

SERENA LYNN ESTES

LifeRich PUBLISHING®

LifeRich Publishing is a registered trademark of The Reader's Digest Association, Inc.

LifeRich Publishing books may be ordered through booksellers or by contacting:

LifeRich Publishing
1663 Liberty Drive
Bloomington, IN 47403
www.liferichpublishing.com
844-686-9607

Because of the dynamic nature of the Internet, any web addresses or links contained in this book may have changed since publication and may no longer be valid. The views expressed in this work are solely those of the author and do not necessarily reflect the views of the publisher, and the publisher hereby disclaims any responsibility for them.

Any people depicted in stock imagery provided by Getty Images are models, and such images are being used for illustrative purposes only. Certain stock imagery © Getty Images.

Scripture quotations are taken from the New King James Version. Copyright © 1982 by Thomas Nelson, Inc. Used by permission. All rights reserved.

ISBN: 978-1-4897-4248-3 (sc)
ISBN: 978-1-4897-4247-6 (hc)
ISBN: 978-1-4897-4249-0 (e)

Library of Congress Control Number: 2022911306

Print information available on the last page.

LifeRich Publishing rev. date:   07/15/2022

# CONTENTS

# PREFACE

We are holy, but we are constantly being sanctified for his use.

> Give thanks in all circumstances for this is God's will for you in Christ Jesus
>
> (1 Thess. 5:18)

Pain increases capacity for life.

*Serenity Prayer:*

★Acceptance
★Courage
★Wisdom

We need to have the courage to accept the things we cannot change, but also have the wisdom to know the difference of what we can change. I think we all can get stuck on wanting to try to control what we cannot change and not take the time to learn how to do the work to change the things we can control. We can gain wisdom by reading scripture and discovering the lessons that we are taught during our life to learn how to accept our trials and tribulations we experience as an opportunity to grow and improve our lives.

My spiritual name is *Shanti Japa Kaur.* The definition of my name is, "Graceful princess/lioness who, by remaining immersed in the meditative repetition of God's name, embodies a peaceful spirit in the world."

*Shanti* means peaceful and tranquil spirit.

*Japa* refers to one who is immersed in continual repetition. One who continuously repeats and meditates on the name of God (Nam).

*Kaur* refers to a lioness. Kaur is recognized as "Princess" or "Spiritual Princess"

My spiritual name has the meaning of "The gift of gracefully personifying a tranquil spirit on earth by perfecting the constant repetition of God's divine name". I feel blessed to have been given this name by the Lord and hope that throughout my life I will continue to have the tranquil and peaceful spirit that God created me to have. I believe the practice of Holy Yoga and learning how to meditate and study scripture has given me this peace within myself. When we meditate with each breath, we experience the profoundly calm energy of oneness with the vibration of the Holy Spirit. He brings warm peace and joy to the minds and hearts of those who learn how to meditate.

I have learned to meditate, exercise, practice yoga, speak in my tongues, love others unconditionally, and just be content. I have hurt many people in my life with the choices that I have made and have asked forgiveness.

I was once told that my work for Christ is used through my speaking and job positions. I have worked in the high tech field over 25 years and it has given me the opportunity to speak publicly and learn the communication skills needed to sell products and services.

Our bodies can be a blueprint of what we have experienced, and I will share with you some of the ways that I have been able to use the tools for healing to help others also find inner-peace and self love to live a life of purpose and understanding of yourself and others.

One Heart | Finding Joy & Peace After Trauma

Serena

E S T E S

Serena hosts Holy Yoga retreats on a quarterly basis and teaches private trauma yoga sessions at her home. She is also a public speaker and shares her story to help others discover healing from their own trauma, loss of loved ones and health issues.

Scripture References:
Women of Faith Devotional Bible
New King James Version Copyright 1982 by Thomas Nelson
YouVersion Holy Bible App

# DEDICATIONS AND RECOGNITIONS

I would like to personally thank a few special people in my life that have helped to guide me, counsel me, and help direct me to the right path. I have learned how to love myself, and stop the madness of self-destruction. My desire is to help others by sharing about the tools that I have found to stop this destruction, and lead a productive, positive and healthy life.

I have had a few counselors who have helped to guide me for the past ten years after the loss of a job. I now have found peace within myself, have addressed my own childhood abuse, and found true faith.

I worked with a spiritual counselor I found after moving back to California after yet another divorce, guiding me in the hurt I experienced, learning to look within myself and find my own soul with a true understanding of having faith and love for myself and others.

The Holy Yoga Foundation and my certification has helped me find this faith-based practice and peace in sharing my story, teaching Holy Yoga, and hosting retreats to help others that have also suffered from trauma and loss.

Lisa Nugent is my best friend in Texas. She has walked by my side for over 20 years after the sudden loss of my husband, a divorce, and the hurt that I have experienced from my own self-sabotage. Lisa is still holding my hand and welcoming me into her home for holidays and truly being my sister from God.

Jayne Clark of *Jayne Clark Coaching* is an Energy Medicine Coach who helps people heal past trauma, grief and loss, as well as recover from addictions. Her work assists her clients in gaining deep emotional well being, mental clarity, and spiritual wisdom.

I met Jayne in Austin, Texas, after losing the love of my life, my third husband, Biff. We were only married five and one half months before he suddenly left this earth. Jayne has given me the perspective from the spiritual side and brought me comfort from loved ones that have left this side of life and are now in the spirit. Jayne also loves wildlife and learning Native American and Shamanic practices. Jayne shares about her gifts here in human form to help us learn from nature, wildlife, and the peace we can find within our soul.

Kimberley Loska, my speaking coach of *As A Heart Speaks*, helped me recognize my heart for public speaking. We met in the children's ministry and had an instant connection. Kimberley's story will inspire multitudes of people. She is a woman of endurance and an author, life coach, and a true friend to me. She has encouraged me in my public speaking and I received my first speaker's reel with her with the *Arras Sisters*. We will be hosting public speaking events and workshops to share our story and help others who have also suffered from trauma and loss.

# PREFACE

Serena's first book published was entitled, *God's Test Pilot*. It is a story of her testimony and description of the various trials, loss and trauma that she had experienced in her first 40 years of life. Serena has the desire to continue to share her story, host public speaking events to help others, and teach Holy Yoga. Holy Yoga is a practice that can help people that have also experienced trauma.

Our state of ourselves is so important. We are not fully responsible for what has happened to us in the past if it was something we could not control, but we can take the experience and learn from it, and train ourselves to change when we approach various circumstances. We do not have to be a product of our environment.

Serena hosts retreats quarterly on the West Coast to include workshops, prayer, meditation, fellowship and relaxation. The workshops are taught on various topics such as Joy, Patience and Endurance. The retreats are hosted by Serena and her two fellow Holy Yoga instructors, Sharon Bernard and Karen Koczwara of Orange County. You can find more information on local retreats at www.serenaestes.com. Oasis Holy Yoga has a private facebook site to find more information on upcoming retreats. Please inquire on Serena's website.

Serena enjoys living in Southern California. She loves the outdoors, the ocean, the mountain air and the desert. Serena has the desire to take her story public. She shares about the tools she has learned with others, and how they can also use their story to help others by describing how they were able to move past hurts. Serena is authentic, vulnerable and speaks truth.

In this book, The White Picket Fence, this is an inspirational and self help book set in Texas and California by Serena who's endured many types of trauma and wants to share her tools for healing with others. Serena continuously sought out the wrong partners, friendships and workplaces and endured many health struggles to try to find this alleged "white picket fence", or ideal lifestyle.

Serena will share with you her struggles in relationships, parenting, enduring health issues, and share stories that women have had in the workplace. Serena will share how she has found tools to help her endure various challenges and lead a productive and healthy lifestyle after much self destruction and the wrong choices.

At age 54, Serena is now in a place where she believes she can share the tools that she has learned and help others who have also made some of the similar wrong decisions

# ONE

# Life Lessons

The main purpose of our lives is to love. Jesus taught us to love like him, which is a difficult thing to do when circumstances and people hurt us here on this earth.

I feel blessed to have had all the opportunities to meet friends, travel, live in different places, and—most of all—have a relationship with God. I believe I am growing spiritually at this time of my life and am finally able to accept the challenges and hurt I have experienced without judging other people.

I have had various types of therapy to release many of the hurtful experiences I have encountered throughout my life, particularly loss. I am now at a point where I can look at all my experiences and learn from them, be self-compassionate, and accept and embrace my trials.

I've had to learn to relax, meditate, and clear my mind. I have learned about the energies of my body and how I can focus on positive aspects. I particularly enjoy my quiet time with God in the mornings. I have learned to release the desire to always have things be perfect in my home and no longer focus on constantly cleaning and being in a hurry. It has taken me many years to learn to look within and accept where I am, and that it's OK to just be still. I have learned to enjoy it. I am able to sleep and rest when I need to, and I thank God every day for the ability to do so.

Forgiveness of our past choices and healing from previous trauma we've experienced in this lifetime is so important. Forgiveness is the only way to move on to the next level of a positive future. We can learn how to forgive and then help others envision positive futures for themselves. It is not healthy to stay stuck in our pasts; we must move forward to our next journey and continue learning. We must listen to the Holy Spirit and his messages to us.

In 2019, I received certification in Holy Yoga trauma training. I was able to provide tools for students to begin healing and integrate psychiatric care with techniques on how to experience a higher quality of daily living after experiencing trauma in their lives.

Trauma almost always involves someone coming after you with something you cannot control. We need to learn how to be resilient. Brooke Boone, the founder of Holy Yoga, states, "If it's not good, it's not over!" I have studied Brooke's teachings and recommend the book *Eat this Book: A Conversation in the Art of Spiritual Reading* by Eugene H. Peterson. We read this book as part of our curriculum to obtain our Holy Yoga certification.

In order to move forward, we need to integrate the Holy Spirit to bring us back into our bodies. Many people continue to live outside of their bodies and don't take the time to recognize we are existing souls in human bodies. The human flesh is a shell that holds our soul within our being. I have learned how to recognize the Holy Spirit inside my body when I envision him into my being. The Holy Spirit gives us messages in so many ways. I have experienced many lessons from dreams and visions, while speaking in tongues, and through prayer.

I truly believe the Lord God has brought different people into my life to send me messages that clarify the purpose he wants for my life. The trick is to stop and listen. It's important to remove yourself from any noisy surroundings or socializing and be alone with yourself to listen to your inner voice.

Our story matters. The Holy Spirit has proposed that humans be partners in the healing of the world. Our bodies are a blueprint of what has happened to us in our lives. For example, I was physically abused as a young child and have continued to remain apprehensive, inhibited, and insecure within my own body, as I did not feel safe.

Trauma is created when one experiences or witnesses a deeply distressing or disturbing occurrence. No one gets to qualify anyone else's traumatic experiences; we all fall in different places on the spectrum. After experiencing trauma, we need to learn how to feel safe in our own bodies. One who has been traumatized can be skeptical with their own awareness. Our senses and feelings are brought to our attention during our yoga practice. We have natural processes in our bodies that get stuck in traumatic experiences. We lack feelings of safety, and we need to do neurobiological work to heal. We need to go through the process ourselves, and we cannot help others who have experienced trauma if we haven't done the healing for ourselves. "Reserve me oh God, for in you, I put my trust" (Psalm 16:1–9).

When people have done the work to help themselves move into healing states of mind and have learned the proper tools to help them feel safe and secure in their own bodies, they can potentially share about their experiences of transitioning from feelings of being unsafe and skeptical of their own senses after experiencing trauma in their lives. The key is, people need to do the mental and physical work to move past traumas into healthy minds and bodies. I have learned to accept my own body and not abuse myself by sharing it with men who do not love or respect me.

The following list includes example of resilience factors that can help a person learn to have a positive experience moving past trauma into a healthier state of being.

Resilience factors can include:

1. spiritual beliefs,
2. family support,
3. viewing struggle as opportunity for growth,
4. gratitude,

5.  having a sense of purpose,
6.  general sense of fortitude in life.

When we choose survival mode after trauma, we continue feeling unsafe. We need to use grounding techniques and breathwork to be in the moment and experience the tools we need to move past states of survivorship into thriving in our daily lives and feeling safe in our own bodies. If we spend time envisioning pleasant sounds and smells, it can make a difference in each moment.

God gives us breath. Breath is inventive and life-giving. His presence comes into our physical being. We have an internal sense of safety when we know where the source of truth is coming from. It is a gift to wake up and breathe. If we allow God to align our days when we awaken, it makes a difference in how we will work through the challenges of our daily lives.

Upon awakening, take the time to just breathe for three minutes. God uses your sufferings to help you transform yourself. (James 1:2) Consider it a sheer gift, friend, when tests and challenges come at you from all sides. You know that, under pressure, your faith is forced into the open to show its true colors, so don't try to get out of anything prematurely. Let it do its work so that you become mature and well-developed, not deficient in any way.

We all want and need more peace. I have studied body symbology, which helps explain the direct correlation between specific health issues. One example from the study of body symbology is when a woman experiences female problems, it can be a direct correlation to -relationship issues.

For example, I experienced severe pain in my life due to endometriosis, fibroids, cysts, scar tissue, and painful cycles. I have had over fourteen surgeries. This could have been attributed to the wrong relationship choices I had made for myself.

I experienced unconsciousness that was unexplained and many other health challenges. I believe my environment and choices have contributed to a great deal of the pain and suffering I have had in my life. I believe there is a correlation between the physical pain I have experienced and selecting the wrong partners in my life and intimate relationships that did not fulfill my desire to have more peace in my life.

I have had many homes in my life, and location was always of great importance. I've always wanted to have quiet and beautiful surroundings. I particularly feel most at peace when I live by the ocean. I love the mountains and desert too and enjoy the air in these physical surroundings. This is who I am. I love nature, raccoons, birds, the sun and ocean, fresh streams and rivers and lakes. This is where I find my inner peace.

My favorite part of living in Texas was listening to the insects chirping, watching the fireflies light up in the summer nights, listening to the rain at night, and feeling the air after tropical storms. It gave me pleasure to view the hill country of the Austin, Texas, area and appreciate the beauty God had created. The people were authentic and friendly. The biggest blessing to me in those years in Texas were the special friends I met who supported me during the loss of the love of my life, Biff, my husband.

I had the pleasure of playing tennis and swimming at the pool at Cimarron Hills Country Club in Georgetown, Texas. Biff, my late husband, loved playing golf while I played tennis. I felt cherished, special, loved, and spoiled while I experienced this part of my life.

I lived in Texas for almost fourteen years. There are many good memories—and some that are very difficult for me to process. God always has a plan, and I continue to focus on that fact to help heal the emotional pain when I think of the losses I have endured. The death of my husband, Biff, was one of the most difficult tragedies I have ever encountered. Although my father died suddenly, Biff and I had a spiritual connection that I feel so blessed to have had in the short time when I was with him.

I was given the opportunity to be part of a Christian grief camp for children. It is called *Camp Agape* and is located in Texas. I found this camp from a magazine advertisement when Biff died, and it immediately appealed to me as an opportunity to give back to children who have also lost loved ones.

Camp Agape is held once a year in Central Texas and has several therapeutic activities that give the children the ability to experience equine therapy, play games, journal, hear music, dance, sing, swim, fish, participate in ropes- courses, hear testimonies, and simply just be with other children that have experienced loss in their lives as well. I have been a part of this camp for over eleven years and served on the Board of Directors. Although I relocated to Southern California, I have stayed involved in this ministry as it speaks to my heart.

I have seen transitions in children that came in angry, scared, confused, and to feel accepted, learning to pray and be vulnerable to their loss.

Fundraising is not my strong suit, but God had challenged me with this ministry in organizing different events and trying to solicit support and recognition for our camp. God has blessed me with this opportunity.

The culture in Texas was different for me. I did not choose to move to Texas. The father of my children and I agreed on this transition from California to Texas. We both believed it would be a good place for us to raise our children. An example of the culture difference between living in Southern California and Texas, entails people displaying dead animals on the wall and enjoying the sport of hunting. In California, I did not meet very many people that enjoyed this sport, and did not see deer displayed in many Southern California homes. I like live animals in the house, and had a difficult time listening to various people discussing the sport of hunting. I love wildlife and domesticated animals and felt like I was living in the wrong culture and I had difficulty relating to these topics of conversation.

The most positive experience I had living in Texas was meeting Biff. Biff was a man that was brought into my life who truly loved me unconditionally, trusted me, respected me, and loved my children. Biff and I would be in the presence of each other and completely content with one another without having to say anything. Biff had also lived in California and also enjoyed the beach and watching the wildlife. We would enjoy sitting on our deck and listening to the birds in the morning.

The short three years of my life with Biff taught me several things. Biff had a saying, "character counts." I can now say that I hear that saying so many times in my head when experiencing difficulty with challenging people and during difficult times with my children.

After the death of Biff, I went into depression. My kids also loved Biff, but I knew we had to move forward. We had moved into Biff's home and were breaking ground on our dream home on five acres. We had selected all the beautiful upgrades and a beautiful lot in a subdivision of Leander, Texas, called Crystal Falls. We were going to have the opportunity to live in the most beautiful part of North Austin. I was crushed to lose this dream when he passed away. I was able to obtain my deposit returned for the home that we were building the next evening after Biff's death. What a blessing to not have to worry about losing the money.

I contacted the bank that Biff had his loan at to try to assume the loan and they were not cooperative. I did not want to have to move my children again. I pulled my bootstraps up and once again, began looking for another home. My poor kids had moved so much due to my divorce from their father, then relocating to another home, and once again when I got married to Biff. I chose to move into the neighborhood near their father and the elementary school they were attending so as not to disrupt their schooling and establish friendships they had acquired since preschool.

The Lord blessed us with the perfect home in a new subdivision in Georgetown, Texas.

Upon arriving in the neighborhood, I asked if there were any three-bedroom homes with an office that did not have other homes behind the backyard, and as luck would have it, there was an existing home that was just perfect for us. I was able to contact the developer due to Biff's relationship and receive a substantial decrease in the price of the home. God always has a plan.

I knew I would need residual income that I would have for my children and college funds for them moving forward. I struggled with fear of not being able to provide for my children.

I had scheduled a garage sale prior to Biff's death and was able to keep my scheduled date. The garage sale was a point of contention with the local community. The locals were making an assumption I would be selling all Biff's belongings and trying to make money. This could not have been further from my plan, and I was so hurt by these people. This is one of the disadvantages of living in a small community.

Love enables us to be in fellowship with people who don't agree with us.

From personal experience of having lost my own father suddenly, I knew Biff's son would need to have all of Biff's personal belongings, although he may not have been ready to handle the emotions of picking them all up. Biff also had three sisters and his father and wife that were understanding and helped me clear out the home. I packed all of his things with great despair in knowing this was the last of Biff's home I would have in my life. His son had his own mother and family to help comfort him, and shortly afterward married a sweet young lady at the country club Biff and I attended.

I was pleased to have helped find this beautiful venue for them to take their vows. Biff and I had also taken our own vows at this same location less than one year prior. The emotions were very strong for me, but I knew it would have been what Biff wanted and it was a blessing to his son. I wanted to be a good, loving person and show his son and family that I could put myself aside and show Christ's love of giving back.

I have had many different types of people in my life with various personalities, beliefs, hurts, challenges, addictions, careers, education, and authenticity. I choose to try to accept those that have experienced different backgrounds, to learn and listen to try to better understand their viewpoints and how to accept that not everyone thinks or reacts the same.

There was a great deal of hurt with false accusations, assumptions about me, and people gossiping about me in the community, considering I did obtain some life insurance from Biff after only being married to him for a short time. It was hurtful, and I will never forget the pain I had in knowing I was doing everything I could to just put one foot in front of the next in my grief.

I was able to use this money to pay off my car and put a down payment on a home that I wanted for my kids in order for them to obtain as stable an environment as possible. The good news in all this was that my kids were still at the same school. Life could move on in a positive way, in a wonderful and safe neighborhood with new friends.

I have learned that we can be the cause of our own problems. If we can lean away from the mess and stay quiet, this gives us reality and allows us to seek freedom, which is the state of well-being. True freedom is freedom from yourself.

# TWO

# Work Relationships

I have worked in corporate America for all of my career and had a challenging sales position at the time of Biff's death. My company gave me three paid days off for bereavement and I had to use all of my vacation that I had accumulated for the total of two weeks that I took off in order to grieve, plan a funeral, and try to get my kids and myself stabilized and look for another home.

When a person experiences sudden loss, it can be difficult to accept that you are part of a company with policies in place when you are dealing with grief and just want to catch your breath and have the time needed to sort things out in your life. This is just one example of the emotions that I have experienced in working for a company that I tried to make my "family". It is important to accept the fact you are an employee, not a family member. I have struggled with feelings of being rejected.

In the void of not having a family, I would try to create my own family unit within the companies that I had worked for in the past, instead of viewing my job as a means to earn and live and pay my bills. My fellow employees were helpful in bringing me meals and were there to listen when I needed to talk, which I am very grateful for.

The environment of corporate America can be self-serving and all business, not personal. This is disheartening to me. I know I'm making a general statement, but the sudden loss of Biff gave me the opportunity to step back and realize that no matter who I work for, I need to keep it in perspective. My fellow employees and boss were both supportive to me at this time.

Working in corporate America is not for a weak person. I have found that I have had to turn the other cheek while being discriminated against, judged, laughed at, propositioned and cheated. I am now choosing to take all that I have learned and not compromise my belief in honesty, hard work, integrity, and the ability to listen to people, discover their actual needs, and help them gain more knowledge about a product or service they need.

One example that a friend had shared with me while working in corporate America was that she had worked with a man that she had known for a number of years and at one point he motioned for her to come into an office in the building to have a physical encounter with him. She felt embarrassed, and betrayed. This was someone she had known for years and that she thought was a friend. She was devastated. She shared with me that she could not believe this person was putting her in such an awkward position. This is just one experience of harassment that women encounter working in corporate America. It is so important to keep boundaries as women working in male dominated industries.

After my friend refused to have this affair, she was told that she could not travel in the field and would have to make eighty outbound calls per day, punch a time clock, and only take one hour for lunch working in a field sales position. She was unable to attend her kids' elementary school lunches or holiday events. Her son still reminds her of this fact. It hurt their relationship.

My friend felt like a punished child working for this company. It can be hurtful to work with people that *appear to be* genuine and care about our careers and truly want us to persevere. As women in the sales environment, we can bring in multiple new customers and still feel like a failure. We can be treated like we are unworthy. Discrimination is still in existence.

I have tried to be as good of a mom as I could be with a demanding career, but only had my kids every other week so I was continually trying to fill my time trying to be happy and feel loved. I believe I continued to look for love and success in the wrong places due to suffering from grief and having an identity crisis. My children also suffered from the loss of their stepfather and watching their mom grieve.

There are good companies to work for, but we must not rush into making the decisions of who to work for and take our time also interviewing the culture and leadership of the companies that we are interviewing to represent. My career has been very important to me, and I have made the mistake of not giving myself the time to assess the right culture conducive to my personality and work ethic.

I started working in corporate America at the age of eighteen for a commercial lending office as a receptionist. I went to college in the evenings and worked for Dee Nelson, who would become the surrogate grandma for my boys twenty years later. During this position working in lending, I felt appreciated, was eager to learn, and responsible.

My jobs I have had in Corporate America since the age of 18 have brought me joy and sorrow.

Dee Nelson was a smart, kind and patient woman that took me under her wing and hired me at such a young age in banking. Dee gave me the experience of respecting and learning from a woman that showed me how to work in a professional environment and extended her love to me after my father died suddenly while working at this company.

Dee was the first person at my home to give me a hug and show me support and comfort. Dee assured me it was acceptable to take time off work after losing my father suddenly. This position also gave me the ability to learn about real estate lending. This was a positive experience I had at the onset of working in corporate America.

After two years in the lending industry, our company closed its doors in the downturn of the savings and loan crisis of 1988 and

I accepted another position as an administrative assistant at another financial company, *BrooksAmerica*. I enjoyed learning about the financial industries, stock market and working in an administrative position meeting many different people.

I continued to attend college and work towards obtaining my degree and switched to another position working for a man with what we will call "the crazy, sleepless boss." This man would come into the office at 1:00– 2:00 a.m. and work continuously throughout the night until the staff would arrive at 8:00 a.m. It was then that his screaming and throwing files at us would begin. He was an unhappy, mean, and frustrated individual. I lasted one year, and moved on to work at the Broadway department store, in cosmetics. I also worked cleaning houses and at a tennis center and catering during the weekends to support myself.

I obtained my bachelor's degree after eight years of attending college and working diligently, attending school at night. I worked many hours. This time of my life was tiring, but I was young, vibrant and focused on getting through school to increase my income and find a suitable career for myself.

After I graduated college in 1994, I was presented with an opportunity in the electronics industry to work in telemarketing to build business for one specific manufacturer while representing an electronic distributor in the semiconductor industry. In one year, I was promoted to a field sales representative for an electronic component distributor. I was offered $36k/year and thought I had reached my dream job. This was the most fulfilling and enjoyable job I have had working in corporate America. I built great long term relationships, learned how to sell, negotiate and had the ability to travel throughout Southern California and felt appreciated and recognized.

I continued to work at this company for six years, obtaining President's Club awards, top sales, and enjoying the drive of field sales and "winning." I felt appreciated and respected at this time of my career.

I have had some difficult relationships working in corporate America. I believe in any work position, you will have the ability to build relationships as well as break them down. It is unhealthy to allow bad relationships to affect you.

I have had bosses that have thrown files at me, yelled and screamed, falsely accused me of disclosing information so that they could get a promotion, and some of my male superiors have propositioned me to have inner-relations with them. I have worked in predominantly male dominated industries. I have a strong personality and can be viewed as too pushy. It is important to understand your own personality, your strengths and weaknesses and find the right fit at the right company.

In the sales environment, I thrive on the challenges and sometimes allow myself to get triggered with the situations I cannot control. It is imperative to not allow ourselves to get caught up in situations at work that are counterproductive to completing our tasks at hand.

Some people have a tendency to just master their jobs and get bored. We need to learn to be at peace and content. It is a job, not the actual purpose in life. I have learned how to stop myself from reacting too quickly. I do not allow what someone says or how they act towards me at work to affect me any longer. I own my own decisions and reactions. It is counterproductive to allow yourself to be in an emotional state during a difficult task or conversation at work.

My favorite parts of sales are solving a problem for a buyer, building relationships, and specific to the electronic industry, working with design engineers and being a part of designing a product and witnessing the end product go into production with the medical, industrial, military, and various market segments.

A large part of selling electronic components entails selling supply chain solutions. The manufacturing of electronic products has migrated predominantly into Asia, where it is less expensive to produce the products. This has affected those of us that spend time with the designers here in America. The culture in Asia is different from America, and it has changed the way we get paid for our design and supply chain efforts.

Working as a commission salesperson, it has been difficult to watch this migration and has been discouraging.

I have struggled with the vulnerability of depending upon feeding my family on an income that has diminished significantly.

On May 3, 2015, I received a vision/dream. I believe this dream was given to me to help me to focus more on my family, not on my job. This dream began with me visiting with my mom and having a discussion about my future and career path. We were laughing and trying to identify a way to find the right position for me. It was like I was picking different ideas from a box with Mom and what I remember selecting is a suggestion, "Time for Change" Serena. This is all I can remember.

During this dream I was then brought by an angel into an elevator. My feet were not touching the floor. It was clear we were going up and I was flying. The elevator opened and we entered several rooms and were flying through. I was given a vision of a yellow Hawaiian dress displayed that I had worn as a child.

The surroundings were beautiful; older tapestries, and different pottery was placed throughout the rooms. It was like a vision of history.

We then came upon a hall with curtains. The angel motioned for me to go to the end of the hall. Each room had white, flowing curtains. The feeling was serene and quiet and warm.

Upon arriving at the end of the hall, I turned right and entered the room. There was my father, lying in bed with his back towards me. I did not recognize him at first, but then he turned towards me, smiled, and laughed. I said, "I can't believe it! It's you! Finally!!" We embraced, laughed, and I woke up.

My father had also struggled with workaholism and was an entrepreneur his whole career. He worked as a real estate agent, contractor, and owned various beauty shops in Hollywood. He was a hard worker as well as an artist and well respected in our community that I grew up in Joshua Tree.

During the dream of my fathers visit, I could feel the Holy Spirit in the room with me upon awakening. It was peaceful, warm, and I felt surrounded by angels.

I cried for at least an hour upon awakening from this dream and the visitation of my father. This is the first time I had seen him in a dream since he died when I was 18 years old. What was the message? I know I have continued to focus on my career my entire life as my identity. The Lord was showing me purpose and focus.

The second thing that was revealed to me in my dream had the spiritual meaning of a message to have courage, faith, and trust in the angels' messages to me. We need to understand how our prayers are manifesting, although it may not be obvious immediately. It may be the test of our patience, but rest assured that it will come to pass in divine time.

It has been revealed to me that job titles don't matter, it is the contentment and opportunity that presents itself with the position that you have either working for yourself or for another company that allows you the freedom to be yourself, be authentic, and help those working with you.

In August 2020, I made the decision to depart from another company, as I did not see the long-term success financially or professionally for me to continue to provide for myself. It was a hard decision, as I really enjoyed the people I worked with and did feel like I was supported, but spent 99 percent of my time cold-calling customers as a seasoned salesperson, and this was a challenge for me.

It can be disheartening to continue to be rejected when you know what you have to sell and knowledge of the industry could benefit these potential new customers, but they are not in agreement of giving you a chance to do business together. I prayed and was called by a competitor to come to work with an existing account base and solid financial package, including 401(k) benefits and a good health plan.

Networking is key in career advancement. I found that during my interviewing process, my rolodex is what hiring managers were interested in when it came to a sales position.

Transferable skills are also key. It is so important to know how to compose a professional resume that can highlight your strengths and key accomplishments. I found myself rehearsing my success stories to reiterate to hiring managers and interviewers.

I have struggled with workaholism in wanting to prove to myself and others that I can be the top producer, obtain the award of being a member of President's Club, and make a substantial income. I wanted my daddy to be proud of me from "the other side".

The choices I have made in focusing on being recognized and earning a certain income has not proven to make me happy. I have also experienced various health challenges by not choosing balance, but work first. It is important for us to remain grateful that we have employment to help us with our livelihood to pay our bills, but to keep the priority of work and life balance.

The electronics industry has given me the ability to learn more about people, specifically buyers and engineers. It has been rewarding, challenging, and taught me patience, how to be more strategic, and learn technical product knowledge.

I believe that in corporate America, women need to show their strength and work very hard to earn respect and be taken seriously in their contribution to the company they represent. In many cases, I have been told to back down, not state my opinion, and learn to let the man take control. In the majority of the meetings and conferences I have attended, I have been the only female. I was told by a friend, "If you are not invited to the conference table, pull up a folding chair!"

During my experience of working for a company, my standard protocol for an out-of-office email would state, "Please stop and read this message." I received complaints about my abrupt approach to communication and that I needed to soften my emails.

The culture was different for me working for this particular company, as I was used to stating my mind, and this gave me the realization that I could be *too* honest, and be judged as a cold person. I am not cold. I am a hard worker, committed, and a dedicated employee.

This was a lesson for me to stop and understand the culture of the company that you work for prior to accepting the position. I made the wrong decision.

This was not the culture or environment for me to work in, yet I continued to create this story of it being the right fit for me, as I had climbed the corporate ladder. It is important to listen to your intuition at all times and not force people into working at your speed.

I have a strong personality, direct in my communication, and knew that the culture for this work environment was not going to be conducive to my personality. It was time to move on. We came to a mutual agreement that the employment contract was not working. I was devastated, and did not want to give up, but knew it was the right decision for both of us. Yes, it was time to move on, but on *my* terms!

This experience of working in this challenging position was a blessing in disguise. God always has a reason and his hand in the cards we are dealt. I now realize the position has brought out the worst in me, struggling with my impatience and negativity.

I wanted to take time to search for the right company to represent for a career. My friendships were so helpful to me during this time of reflection and soul searching. I spent time with friends, enjoyed time at the beach, and time with my son.

This time of my life in between jobs gave me the opportunity to do more spiritual reflection, seeking counsel for career coaching, and reading about different careers that could potentially fulfill my dream of helping others that have suffered loss of loved ones.

After over 20 years in corporate America, I am now in a position to use my strengths in the ability to sell and take all of my personal experiences and sell my products and services to various people all over the world teaching them how life experience can help us in every facet of life to live for peace, understanding, love, and the true meaning of the purpose of life.

God has given me more clarity each year of my life to seek within and discover the joy in all experiences of life, whether they are in suffering or challenges that have been thrown my way. It is all for the good. There is always a purpose.

My main goal for a career for myself is to work for the right type of company that will allow me to communicate positively, learn how to improve myself with support from my superiors, obtain the flexibility for my personal time, receive the monetary compensation needed to provide for my family, and plan for my retirement. Work and life balance is key.

We need to construct ourselves by our own personal values. I believe we need to be the best person we will ever be with authenticity, and not worry about fitting in. In the world of corporate America, I struggle with not just saying what is on my mind and having to adjust my personality and watch my P's and Q's in my interaction with others.

Our Lord has a way of revealing how we can be humble during career and relationship transition. I have spent many years of my life trying to prove to myself and others that I am worthy, when all along, truth is what matters. I am competitive, and have always worked in a sales position.

I had the opportunity to meet a fellow colleague in my industry that helped me face this truth that I was ignoring all along. She gave me some exercises to do deep breathing and looking deep into the mirror and telling myself, "I love you."

I know it is important to step into our fears and know what they are. Where we are today needs to be the focus.

I have had a great run in the electronics industry for over twenty-five years, obtaining a six-figure income and having fun, traveling throughout the states and other countries, including Mexico, Canada, and Germany. I am appreciative of the opportunity to learn, develop my technical knowledge, and meet great people. I often ask myself, "What do I want for my future?" After working in the same industry all of these years, it takes courage to leave and find another way to make a living. We stay with what we know.

My heart's desire has always been to help others who have also suffered the loss of loved ones—widows, and children of alcoholics—by sharing my story. I have the desire to be well respected and thought of as a kind person.

There are times when I look back at what my personality and reputation have been, knowing that suffering has built my self-confidence. I need to address the fear of the unknown, of leaving the familiar to reach the ultimate goal of finding who I really am.

I enjoy hosting yoga retreats, teaching Holy Yoga, and facilitating workshops and public speaking sharing my story of how I have found contentment and peace after loss, abuse, tragedies, and health issues would fulfill a need in me.

In leadership, we need to have the right goals for the right reasons. I often sit and ponder about what the real purpose of my working world should be.

I think many of us spend the majority of our time focused on the objective of making a lot of money, and the key result doesn't always satisfy the soul's desire to fulfill our real purpose on this planet.

If we combine ambition and purpose, we can identify the compelling reason for our goals and understand what our passion really is. We want to accomplish the true goal of making a difference while we are living here on earth, then leave a legacy for our children or others when we move to the other side.

I will continue to work on my anxiety and impatience. I had a session with a spiritual healer that immediately could discern that I have suffered from anxiety my whole life. This has been attributed to the way I had conducted myself both at work and in my family life.

I had not slowed down to listen to God speaking to me within the first 15 years of my career. I have had a tendency to move a million miles an hour and exhaust people around me due to my high level of energy, but struggle with negativity when faced with challenges and negative circumstances. It has taken work on myself to learn how to slow myself down, not take people and their reactions in the work environment personally and enjoy my career.

My answer is within me; God shows us all the challenges will continue to come, but the lessons are always there to teach us how to accept our lessons with grace, gratitude, and understanding. This is what Christ came to teach us on earth.

I am thankful that God has provided the blessing of good-paying jobs, the ability to meet with many people throughout the world and share in my passion of working hard.

In working for the high tech industry for over twenty-five years, I feel prividledged to have had the opportunity to influence others within the industry about accountability and the fact that what gets measured, gets done.

The Lord provides us with the resources to accomplish his purpose for our lives. A lack of resources to accomplish something, even in our purpose, may be God's way of guiding us in a new direction or into moving to a slower paced lifestyle.

I pray that my next chapters for my career will be positive, peaceful, and relaxing. I want to experience the feelings of enjoyment and pleasure, and continue to have faith in knowing that everything will unfold just as it is supposed to. I believe we can weave working in corporate America and our own hobbies into a productive work environment for ourselves. We can learn ways to earn additional income by helping others and using the gifts that God has given to us. The key is to have balance and use our time wisely. We will never change the fact that there are 24 hours in a day.

I believe I have sought out this "white picket fence" of the perfect career and built many relationships in the working world that have been both positive and negative for me, but it is key to keep our working world in perspective. Our careers should be a way to earn a living, build relationships, but it is not our family environment.

# THREE

# Marriage Choices

I was not good about avoiding relationship addiction and loneliness after the sudden loss of my husband in 2011. I contacted an old boyfriend from California to come see me. This man and I had a strong physical desire for each other and went immediately into a physical relationship that lasted nine months. He and I traveled to see each other once/twice per month on the weekends and had fun together. He shipped his motorcycle to my home, and my younger son, Gavin, rode on it with him. I will never forget the look on my son's face riding on this bike in my local neighborhood. He loved it and it made him smile.

After nine months of this love affair, this man said he sold his bike and needed to ship it back to California. He called me the following Saturday after receiving his bike back and stated, "I can't play second fiddle to Biff; I won't be moving to Texas and I don't love you!" Once again, I was in shock and hurt. I should not have chosen yet another relationship with a man that was emotionally unavailable for me, and it was way too soon after Biff's death.

I identify myself to be God's Test Pilot, which is the title of the first book I wrote after Biff's death.

> The reason I entitled the book, "God's Test Pilot" was
> to share about my stories of experiences multiple losses,
> trauma, sickness and using this context of being a "test

pilot" enduring different challenges that have been given to me as life experiences to share about how I was able to move past these tragedies and remain in my faith in Jesus Christ.

(2 Corin 5:7) For we walk by faith, not by sight.

The Lord knows the choices I have made and will make, and He always remains steadfast in his commitment to us and forgives us for our mistakes. Hurt people hurt people, and I have been on the receiving and giving end of it. I have tried to make the commitment to myself that I would not date, would not have any physical relationship, and would work on myself and my kids. At one point I had accepted a job that I thought would be a great opportunity to have time with my kids and work in a sales environment with a company that I thought had integrity.

In 2014, I chose to marry again. Biff passed away on March 24, 2011. I was out with some friends watching a live band and he was standing near us. We proceeded to spend the evening laughing and talking and having fun all together. I immediately exchanged Facebook contact information and heard from him in the next couple of weeks. One of my best friends, Lisa, who understands me, said to me the evening we met, "Serena, you are just going to open up your life to this guy and share Facebook right away? Oh, well, you can always delete him." We laughed. I should have listened, but no, here I went again, to self-destruction, not listening to my intuition to slow down.

The night I met my next partner, he grabbed my hand and stated, "You have been through a lot, I can tell." Well, I certainly had! I felt warm and cared for hearing this comment from him. This man had also encountered loss, had two children of his own, one of which was in college. We began to date and had many good conversations, took weekend trips together, and I believed this to be my opportunity to be loved again. What I did not do was listen to my heart. I knew that my younger son did not like him, and I chose to believe this would change.

Two years into the relationship, we went to Hawaii and got married. I pushed for this, instead of slowing down and taking my time in assessing what was really the right choice for me and my children and our living arrangement. The house I was living in had a home built right up against my backyard, which was the one thing that I did not want to encounter. Passing the Gray Poupon over the fence was not my ideal living arrangement. I took it upon myself to seek out another lot in a beautiful neighborhood and told my future husband I would love for him to be a part of buying this lot and living together, but wanted to be married, since I had two kids and thought it was the right message for them.

Once again, I was not listening! My son was angry and did not like this home. The new home was on a lot backed up to a beautiful reserve with a creek. We selected beautiful white stone, upgraded wood floors, an elegant master bathroom, a large home office for me, and a Jack/Jill bathroom for the boys. I thought this was my new paradise, and I would be happy again. We can search for wells of the wrong living water in materialism, thinking it would fill our hearts.

During the first year of marriage, I had desired to make love, relax, travel, take walks, talk about common dreams, and just be together. We were in such different places. My husband was a business owner and that was his first love, and his children came ahead of me and my two children as well. This was understandable. I knew this when I married him; why didn't I listen to my heart? I created a story of the perfect marriage yet again, not listening to my inner voice that perhaps this was not the best decision for me or my children at this time of my life.

I knew I could not change another man and needed to accept him for who he was and understand his passions.

This man had also experienced his own life challenges, and very much an individualist with similar survival tools that I had in my life. He was hardworking and did have the love of God, but our priorities were different.

The feelings that I experienced were not what I had expected. I created a story that was a fairytale for myself. We both were not fulfilling our love languages. The book entitled, *The Five Love Languages* By Gary Chapman written in 1992 outlines five general ways that romantic partners express and experience love, which Chapman calls, "love languages' '.

I was trying to force another relationship that was not right for me and ignoring the signs being given to me. I chose to make the commitment to marry again even though my partner was on the fence about actually taking that step. I pushed the issue; it is a pattern for me. Why wasn't I listening? I thought it was the right thing to do, building a beautiful home together.

This is an example of trying to create the "white picket fence" in my life. Things changed. My pattern continued, hurting another man in my life.

During the timeframe of building our new home, I was presented with a career opportunity with a manufacturing rep company and was able to work from my home office. My boss was supportive of the time that I needed for my boys, and this gave me the opportunity to get back in the field to sell electronic components. I persevered in this position and obtained awards. The company was a small company and not the right fit for me long term, so I once again felt like I needed to move in another direction.

It was at that time that one of the manufacturers I represented opened a position for me to work with the West Coast in a management position, traveling to all of the beautiful parts of the country that I enjoyed and loved. I could travel the optional weeks that I did not have my kids. I should have asked myself, "Where would that leave my husband?" Our relationship suffered. The communication became less and less, the stress of my son with him became evident to me in knowing it would not change.

After a year in the position with this company, I was given the opportunity to relocate back home to California with my boys. Their father had also stated he wanted to move back "home." I had a decision to make.

I had written many letters and tried talking about my feelings. This beautiful, white stone home felt like living in an igloo for me. The couch talks stopped. I had an opportunity to relocate home to California and my kids' dad wanted to move as well. I'm sure my partner felt abandoned.

Texas was my partner's home, and my expectation for him to come to California with me was unrealistic. I felt like I had made the wrong decision in marrying this man. I loved him, but my kids did not, and I wanted to be home. My relationship was not an unconditional, loving relationship that I had encountered with Biff. I believe this was a rebound for me, and I hurt this man and left him.

My partner at this time owned a business, did not have the same love of animals that I did, and enjoyed hunting and socializing with the neighbors. That is not where I saw myself living. I had made up this story in my mind that this man would take walks with me near our creek, enjoy the Jacuzzi with me, spend time with my kids and show me the same attention I had become accustomed to in having found my true soul mate in Biff, not paying attention to the fact that this was certainly not my reality in this relationship. I had once again rushed into creating an imaginary love affair. I was depressed and felt stuck. I had continual health issues of extreme fatigue, IBS issues, and celiac disease. At one point, the doctors stated that I had an autoimmune disease, most likely Lupus.

I believe in all of my career choices, relationship failures, I had continued to search for love and financial stability in the wrong places.

My point of reference that I had created for myself was to make a lot of money, force myself into relationships that did not reciprocate true love, and caused major health issues for me. I was not taking the time to be patient, stop, listen and be content with where I was working and with being by myself. This caused issues for me and my kids and it was not leading a productive lifestyle. I identified myself as having a "relationship addiction."

I was not seeking God and his direction for my life, but trying to force this physode of the "white picket fence" by living in a beautiful home, personifying being in a loving relationship, and being a mom to my two children that were starving for my attention and love, while watching their mom self destruct in continuing to make the wrong decisions for her life. I have asked for forgiveness from God from these choices that hurt my children and several men that I had chosen as husbands.

# FOUR

# Parenting, Not Easy

When a mother has a child that has issues in school, and arguing with her about any boundaries, it is disheartening. Parenting is not easy. I have tried to instill upon both of my children a positive example for direction and a constructive environment. When a parent experiences a family member struggling, it is a feeling of helplessness. I prayed, "Lord, how do I deal with this?" It is so hard when someone close to you is physically stronger than you and can be an angry person, blaming you for things you cannot control.

As a single mother, I have been disappointed, knowing that the two households were different for my boys, and some of the "friends" in the neighborhood were bad news. It is so hard for kids to have to live in two neighborhoods and households. I created this picture of both of my sons having the opportunity to surf, participate in theater, and find their own passions. I wanted my boys to grow up in a good area and find ways to enjoy themselves and find the right friends.

My boys had trouble getting along with each other, and I felt like a failure as a mother. I felt like I was not a good mother to my children and competing with their father for their attention. I felt lost, confused, and defeated. I cried and began to pray, "Lord, please give me the answers". I felt like I wanted to run away from it all and just give up.

I know there is not an instruction book for parenting, and feel like without having my own parents to help direct me, I was making the wrong decisions on how to parent my children and felt isolated by my younger son.

When a mother experiences a child being sent to a therapeutic boarding school, there is a feeling of defeat and failure. Parents seek therapy and psychiatric care for the family unit to try to obtain direction and guidance on how to help their children. I have reached out to various doctors for the right answers.

The father of my children loves them. I believe neither one of us were shown the tools needed in order to give our sons a home with boundaries and a safe environment away from kids that were giving my struggling son a bad influence. They lived in two different households. I learned that making the agreement to share custody equally during the divorce may not have been the best option for them. Divorce is not easy, especially for the children. I was stuck with my decision of equal custody.

As a mother, I remained consistent with my rules of limited electronics, requesting my boys to go outside to play, eating at the dinner table, doing chores and coming straight home from school. I tried every sport and extracurricular activity for both of my children. My boys are just not team sports kids. I must say, I'm envious of all the perfect-looking, sports-minded families at the ball field, going on vacation together and loving life. That has not been my experience of parenting.

I refuse to give up on my children. I still struggle with the thought of what my child witnessed and endured in the 15 months he spent in boarding school.

I was told there were some occurrences that transpired at a boarding school that could have harmed him both mentally and physically. It is so hard to feel like you made the wrong decision for your child when you thought you were helping them get the help they needed.

At this time of my child attending a boarding school, I knew I would need to obtain a position at a company that would allow me to be there for my son, as well as continue to provide money for his treatment. It was hard to come to the realization that this last position was a promotion for me, but I needed to be mindful of my children's well-being first, as opposed to continuing to climb the corporate ladder.

I read a great book, *Active Pro-Parenting* by James Lucas, to help me with the transition of my son coming home from boarding school. Mr. Lucas states, "Life is not a race of knowledge and credentials, it's a race of godly wisdom and character." Character counts, and corporate politics is everything against my character. I'm honest, direct, true, and hardworking, not political, and want to help others.

As a young child, I was taught that education is a priority and that obtaining good grades is very important to obtain a successful career. My mother came from a family that supported education and it was very important to her family members to attend college.

I was taught that if I would obtain straight A's in elementary school through college, I would have a better income and career.

I always enjoyed school and learning, but I did not retain information when I would study for tests. I had to teach myself how to study. It did not come easy for me with my ADHD brain to slow myself down in school and stop and listen to my teachers. I wanted to fast forward through school.

Jaden, my older son, graduated high school in spring of 2020 and I was so proud. He did not take the usual route in high school and chose to complete his senior year by taking classes online and working a job in addition to saving money for college.

I am so proud of my son Jaden, knowing that he will be an asset to our society by showing others his strength, genuine spirit, and good work ethic. Jaden started at the age of sixteen years old by riding his bike to work as a prep cook in an Italian restaurant, and also was recruited to do catering work on the weekends as well.

My boy is very well-respected and kind in nature. People resonate with Jaden in seeing how hard he works and that he is his own person. He has never been a boy to succumb to what others think he should be. He is an artist and highly intelligent, with his own personality and humor. He likes girls, and probably has spent more of his time with the females of the species than the boys, but the girls appreciate his honesty and care for them.

I am able to trust God in knowing that Jaden will complete college or obtain a certification in a field that he will persevere and be successful for a good company. Jaden is financially responsible and paid me for his car and insurance from the time he was 16 years old.

I believe Jaden will save his money and continue to be frugal and have a balance, knowing that material things are not of importance to be happy in this life. He likes shopping at thrift stores and has said to me that "things" do not matter to him. Jaden did not want me to spend too much money on him, as he didn't need much while he was growing up. Jaden has a kind soul and will be a success in whatever he chooses for his occupation and as a means to take care of himself.

In July of 2020, I bought a home in Canyon Lake, California, and made the choice to move one hour away from Orange County. It was difficult to tell Jaden that I was moving, but knew I needed to start a new life and that he had a place to stay with his dad during college and would always have a room at my home to stay. It was time for me to let go of the reins and let my boy fly and find his own path. Jaden moved with me and paid me rent and went to work in our area.

It was time to surrender to God. I had financed two boarding schools. It is so hard to let go of trying to be in control, especially as a mom when you just want the best for your child, but also knowing you need to set boundaries for yourself.

I pray every day that the people in this world can see the light, knowing that their bad choices are not going to get them very far in life.

I have sought wise counsel from a Christian counselor and friends. I continue to pray for my loved ones, but will not allow my boundaries to be compromised. We all want the people that we love in our lives to be safe and to select the right "friends" to spend time with.

The people we choose to bring into our lives can be based on insecurity and sadness from our pasts. For me, I just accepted as many people into my life as I could, to try to create the "family" that I did not have.

I am in constant prayer for my loved ones to acknowledge that they are loved, protected, and need to make the right decisions in order to avoid legal ramifications and destruction of their bodies. There are so many negative influences in this society for the children growing up in this world today. I know that I need to accept the things I cannot change, and let go of the control.

It is so hard to not get frustrated, depressed, and anxious over the tragedy of a person you want to help not wanting to make the right decisions for their lives. I need to take deep breaths in, pray, and surrender to Christ, as I know the Lord loves everyone even more than I am capable of loving them. I pray the people in this world will reach up, knowing God is there. I can no longer continue to hurt myself and endure more of my own health issues due to anxiety and sadness. I have had to detach with love.

I pray for the day that my children will reach out to others to help them, and that they will find their way. I believe they will both be healed and take a productive direction for their lives, in God's timing.

Someday I hope my children will have the desire to help other teenagers who do not feel secure in themselves. Some teenagers choose drugs, the wrong friends, and disrespect rules and regulations set by their parents that only want to help them.

I know that God has a plan in all this pain, and there will be an opportunity to help others by showing them that I was able to release and let go and trust. Not an easy task. Pain can be profound, but can also be very healing.

I believe I am continuously being encouraged to slow down and not take things too seriously. I need to lighten up and change my perspective about issues and matters that have been on my mind. When I think of young boys attending boarding schools, I believe the parents need to stop and thank God for the ability to have funded these schools to try to help their children.

I sometimes suffer from anxiety in creating the story that my children will not make it through difficult parts of their lives. In prayer, God gives me the clarity in knowing that my loved ones will not self-destruct all of their lives. We all make mistakes, grow up, and learn our lessons. I want my children to learn to make good choices and be a productive part of society. I know that I will need to be encouraging and have a softer approach with my children. (Proverbs 22:6) Train up a child in the way he should go: and when he is old, he will not depart from it.

Some people continue on a destructive path of anger towards others and do not learn from their mistakes. It can be disheartening to watch people you love live in this self-destruction. There was a time of my life where I felt at a loss for answers.

When a loved one tells you they hate you and resent you it is hard to know what to do. I will continue to pray for all of the loved ones in my life. I have felt misunderstood and actually have struggled with feeling guilty and ashamed of my parenting skills.

Motherhood and parenting is the hardest job I have ever had. I feel like I do not make the right decisions, lose my patience, am at a loss for the right words to say, and anxiety takes over inside of me.

During the time that your family is in therapy, the best thing you can do is obtain information for yourself to better understand how you can contribute to providing your loved ones the right environment for them to feel loved. As a child, I had several different therapy sessions where my father tried to help me move past the hurt of losing my mother at such a young age. I have spent time reading Scripture, learning more about myself, the reason for my anxiety and impatience. The Lord has given me several different sources for learning about myself. My main source of education is the Holy Bible.

My therapist helped me to identify my communication skills and how I could improve upon them. It is so hard to not become emotional while being yelled at, deliberately disrespected, judged and feeling depressed. Until we all take ownership of our part in the reason behind the hurt, we cannot move forward.

I had the desire to understand my next steps and how I can move forward with life after the divorce from my childrens' father in a positive manner and letting go of this episode I had created of this perfect "white picket fence" with a healthy family for my children. I regret the hurt that I have caused my children from the divorce of their father, but have forgiven myself and asked forgiveness from them. I know it was in God's plan to bless me with my children.

It is so hard not to want to step into the role of "rescuer" or problem solver when your children are suffering from the loss of family unity. I had to direct my thoughts in a positive manner, knowing that it is not for me to fix it, it is in God's hands. Keeping the faith in this situation is the only solution there is to have. We can spend the time listening to the Lord speak to us in the quietness and studying his word to better understand hurt and the fleshly sin that we encounter.

In 2017, my older son moved with me to California his sophomore year of high school which can be a hard transition. I started attending my old church and taking him to the youth group sessions with a desire for him to select healthy friends and feel accepted in his new environment. Overall my son thrived very well. He is a social, sweet, loving, honest and accepted individual. He is smart and people are drawn to his confidence and ability to not be a follower.

At age sixteen, the hormones started to rage in my son. He became interested in girls. This was so hard for a mom to accept in wanting him to not desire sex at such a young age. I didn't want him to get an STD or impregnate a girl at such a young age. It was good to see him happy and accepted, but difficult for me to try to help him make choices that would be positive for him long-term. I struggled as a teenager seeking love from boys that were not emotionally available to me. My son is a caretaker and was attracted to girls that had emotional issues.

I have also selected the wrong partners in my life seeking out the men that needed direction and help for their own lives.

I had a dream during the time of "COVID" on 8/31/2020. I was in the clouds and there were babies below me. I was saving them in their life. I was teaching them. I was in a mothering and authoritarian position counseling these small children and then I moved into the celestial realm. There was an angel that was showing me there was a baby to save, and we were trying to get to this child. We were searching for this child and could not find it. I then went back to this "angel" and he was possessed..his demeanor had changed.

The angel's eyes were black and red and very frightening and he said he would not let us save this baby. I then started speaking in my tongues and rebuking this evil spirit from this angel and stating, "In the name of Christ " remove this evil spirit. The angel's body went limp. I laid my hands on this angel and he woke up and was light and filled with Christ and back as an angelic form. He showed us where the baby was, and we took it and helped it.

I went back "into flight", with the baby and was able to have the ability to find him and help to save him. I thanked Jesus for the opportunity to save this baby. I then went into another place, coming down an escalator at an airport. I was still with my angel 'friend" and we saw all the people below us and some had halos shining and like head bails. These people smiled at us and I told my angel friend they could see us. We were also glowing. Other people did not have halos and I understood. I woke up from my dream with such joy, power and an exuberant feeling.

This dream took place four days after my son was in a terrible car accident and rolled his car four times down an embankment, totaled his car, and survived with a compression fracture on his back and the two other boys in the car survived with no injuries. It was a miracle. My son did not have to have surgery and did not have any neurological issues. The message of this dream to me was that we all have choices, we can try to save those, but they all make their own choices. When we seek the light of Christ to be an example to others and focus on our purpose to help them, in knowing that it is not our job to select the chosen ones, only our Lord. We are here to be vessels and a light to give others love, safety, encouragement and show them the agape love that God created us to share with others.

The opportunity I have had here in earth school to be a mother has been the most challenging, fulfilling, heartwarming experience I encountered. It has also been the most difficult assignment for me to let go and let God.

I think our Lord speaks messages to us in dreams to give us guidance and clarity as to our lessons that we are to learn from our actions and choices that we make here in our human experience. The Lord spoke to so many prophets through dreams, and still does. It is such a gift to have the interpretation of dreams when you have them, knowing that this time is when you are quiet and still, and if you listen and learn, there are always messages for us in our sleep state with the gift of visions and dreams.

# FIVE

# Hope In Parenting

## Jaden's Song

On September 22, 2001, I gave birth to my first son, Jaden Lee Troutman. He was the apple of my eye, my miracle baby, and I cried when the doctor handed him to me. I cannot even try to describe the delight in my heart when I gave birth to him and she laid him on my stomach. it was funny, we had told the pediatrician that we did not want to know the sex of the child and I was put on bed rest the last month of the pregnancy due to some complications, and during one of the ultrasound she stated, "When you have the circumcism done", I mean, IF you have to have one - well, that gave it away! So when I gave birth to my precious Jaden, she stated, "It's a boy!" He was healthy, seven pounds and eleven ounces, the most precious loving being I had ever laid my eyes on.

The hospital stay was short and I felt a little nervous in not knowing much beyond the parenting classes and reading "What to expect when you're expecting" and with my engineer mind, I read all about putting him on a schedule. I was so diligent with his feeding, naps, and bedtime, he was sleeping through the night at 7 weeks. This made one tired momma happy and more rested. He was well fed, rested and headed on the right path to a productive schedule for his life. He typically stays on a schedule and is diligent with being to work on time and never late to school as a young adult today.

Jaden had his own personality. He would run up to people in restaurants and church and introduce himself, laughing and acting jovial. Jaden is a loving boy with so much character. He had his own method of crawling that we called the "army crawl" with one leg dragging on one side. I made his own baby food and had the pleasure of staying home with him the first five years of his life.

I became involved in the Mom's Club and hosted many playgroups at my home, as his dad built them a playground and beautiful area in the backyard for the kids to play and learn social skills. This was probably one of the most delightful parts of my life, in building relationships with other moms, watching our kids grow together and taking camping trips in our 5th wheel RV. We traveled to many state parks, beaches, mountains and watched the rivers and ocean waves outside of our trailer and Jaden played with his little monster truck toys.

I took Jaden to Gymboree and watched him crawl into the circle many times and laugh and make himself available to be seen by all of his "peers". Not a shy boy, and quite confident with his "gymnastic" skills.

He would stay busy and never seemed to get tired of playing, although mommy got tired!

I tried very hard to stay patient, build a good life for my first boy, and be involved with as many productive activities that I could to build friendships for him and show him structure and love. Jaden's dad worked very hard and owned a construction company, he was so helpful to me and always made sure everything was in order and that he would be there for his son.

Jaden's father is so proud of him and would hold him and tell everyone what an awesome experience it was to have a son and build a good life for him. These were good years for all of us watching Jaden grow into a toddler with his jovial and cheerful personality.

Jaden grew quickly and we got him involved in the YMCA and tried many sports activities, bought him a four wheeler for his size to ride during our camping trips. We also had waverunners that we would take out on the rivers and lakes and had friends with boats that he could ride on inner-tubes and play in the water. It was such a joy to watch my boy at the beach and playing in the sand and building.

Jaden was particularly talented at building cities and different creations with his legos. We had the privilege of living near Legoland, so I got an annual pass and took him and his brother often with friends from the moms club and let the boys play and ride on the boats and build their own lego structures. I knew that my boy had a creative mind and was not necessarily going to be the "sports figure" that some parents think boys should become. This was a good opportunity to allow individuality and watch a personality grow.

We moved to Texas and sold many of the toys quickly afterward, so Jaden needed to find new activities to occupy his time. He liked to play paintball with his friends and video games and on his computer. I was very strict about the games I wanted him playing, music he listened to, and movies he would watch. I wanted so badly to show him the innocence and keep him away from some of the bad influences in this world our kids can be exposed to. It was hard for me to see other families allow different structures in their home.

Parenting is a learning lesson and can be a good opportunity to allow yourself to "let go" and allow your child to be their own individual. Jaden selected a few close friends and stayed busy and did very well in school.

In middle school, Jaden was selected on the honor roll and some of the teachers saw his potential in becoming an advanced student and entered into the IB program his freshman year. His father and I had divorced when he was six years old, and had an alternative week schedule. We made sure we lived close so it would be better for the boys. Jaden made a concerted effort to do well in school and maintain good grades. The IB program was too much for him. This is an advanced education that accelerates the curriculum for high school students and the workload can be five times the pace of a regular high school student. Jaden experienced anxiety, so we transferred him into a different high school and he kept all AP classes which was still causing anxiety for my boy. I knew his potential, but wanted to be mindful of him not experiencing too much stress. He kept a few advanced classes and continued to show interest in graphics arts and computer gaming. He learned how to write code in middle school and was recognized by teachers as being very bright.

When moved to California when Jaden was in his sophomore year of high school he did very well with the transition into Dana Hills High School in an affluent area of Dana Point, CA from a small town named Leander, Texas. It was an adjustment, but Jaden had taken an interest in tennis and played in Texas and continued for a semester in California. He helped in a summer camp, and I enjoyed the time together playing tennis.

Jaden lost interest in tennis and wanted to get a job and a car at age sixteen. He had drivers ed in Texas, but California would not accept his permit and had to start over. He took it in stride, and worked hard to learn to drive and obtained his license at 17 and we got him a car. Jaden started his first job at a restaurant at age sixteen and rode his bike to work and school. I was so proud of my boy and his work ethics and diligence in taking on his own responsibility.

It is with great honor to tell the story of my Jaden and his song that continues in knowing that he will be his own man, and I hope that one day he can look back and know that although I was a mom with structure and had him pay for his own car, insurance and phone, I did it to teach him responsibility and work ethic. I want him to see the opportunity that he had to be responsible at a young age and find friends for his life that will bring him joy and acceptance. The joy of parenting comes when you watch your child grow, laugh, smile, take his first steps, ride his first bike and pay you for his own bills with dignity and honesty in knowing that his hard work will pay off.

## Gavin's Song

Gavin was conceived shortly after Jaden, and he was born nineteen months after our first son Jaden. The pregnancy was difficult and I was put on strict bed rest for five and one half months with Jaden as a baby. We were blessed with my husband's seventeen year old niece, Jennifer, who graduated early from high school and came to live with us to help me with Jaden during the challenge of bedrest.

I had a shortened cervix that caused me to contract every time I stood up. This was a challenging time both mentally and physically for me. Jaden was walking and getting into everything and I could not play with him like a new mother would desire.

Gavin came into the world after thirty seven weeks of pregnancy and we were delighted to have another beautiful healthy boy. It was funny, my friend who was a radiologist had done a scan when I was twenty weeks pregnant, and stated she thought it was a girl. Well, God certainly had different plans. I had many 3D images and weekly visits to the doctor during this high risk pregnancy, and soon found out it was indeed a boy.

Gavin was different from Jaden. He was dependent and wanted to be held close to me. Breastfeeding was such a bond for me with Gavin. I had studied "BabyWise" and stayed diligent with putting him on a schedule and it was so hard, but he did end up sleeping through the night at nine weeks. I felt so blessed to have the ability to once again walk around with my two boys, push them in the stroller, host playgroups and be home with my two boys. Jaden loved his new little brother, it was so cute watching him cuddle him and bring him toys and bottles. His own playmate had arrived. Jaden is so sweet tempered and showed so much love to his brother.

Gavin has a funny personality and can be stubborn, like his momma! He loves animals, babies and nature. He liked the outdoors and building forts. He tried every sport and did well in flag football. Gavin struggled with focus starting in preschool and his father and I divorced when he was four years old. Gavin did not do well with this separation and struggled. I felt so guilty for "breaking up my family", and it was hard to see him cry and ask for daddy.

We agreed to have shared custody with a schedule alternating every other week for equal time with the boys. I went back to work when Gavin was three years old and that was difficult, but we needed an income.

The first incident for Gavin was in a preschool where they left him unattended in a hot bus in August in Texas. I do not know how long he was there, and the school did not inform me of this incident. I received a letter from CPS, as he had been with his father that week, and I was not called to give me the information. When I asked him what happened, he said, "Mommy I was hot and I had to go potty." There is no way a small child would not have been affected by this. The school principal was soon fired and both teachers were also removed from the school immediately. It was so tragic that my son endured this neglect and it is hard to even think about today, but I know God always has a plan and purpose. It is hard to know what it is at the time, but I'm sure it will be revealed in the future.

Gavin enjoyed riding his bike and scooter, and was active. He always found friends and built forts near the house. He and Jaden would play with some of the same friends, but they were definitely their own individuals. Gavin was more outgoing and started taking acting classes in middle school. He did very well and liked being on stage. Gavin has the natural ability to make people laugh and I love his desire to want to entertain people.

I love Gavin so much. He has a strong personality like me, and we can have a difficult time communicating with one another, but we both aspire to make people laugh and help others.

Gavin can light up a room when he is surrounded by others, and I see him using this talent in his future career.

Parenting has been the biggest challenge in my lifetime. My point of reference has been that of neglect, being ignored, having two parents that were not in their right mind the majority of my upbringing, and there was no trust.

My boys know that I love them, but I want them to know I am proud of them. I can remember one time when my father told me he was proud, but was generally concerned about my grades.

I have done the same thing with my sons that my father had done with me as a strict parent. I have pushed them hard in school and focused on trying to make sure they are safe and teaching them to be a good addition to society. My father would always say to me, "Attitude is everything Serena." I know the way that I have communicated to my boys has been direct and may not have been received well as young boys, but I hope and pray that they will understand that my intent was good and out of love for both of them.

School was drilled into my head as a young child and throughout high school, I was taught schooling would be the top priority and grades were going to show this achievement. I did not retain a lot of the information that I did learn, as I programmed myself to memorize to get the grade. I was hyperactive, an only child, and criticized for being spoiled.

My mother's saying to me was, "Oh, EVAY, Serena." She was forty-one years old when she had me, and did not have much patience for a hyper little girl. Her first daughter died at age twelve from an illness. I was planned and a "miracle" child, but was the second child from a woman that hurt deeply from losing her first child to leukemia.

It is difficult when it is challenging to try to talk to and spend time with someone that you love so much. I have struggled with feeling disrespected and felt ashamed, and it is the same emotion I felt towards my parents being alcoholics and disengaged from me.

I have been hard on both of my sons, and know that at times they felt inadequate in school and they both suffered socially. They both have been searching to find their way since infancy.

The experience of sending a loved one away to get the help to try to find the security within themselves can be bittersweet. I pray continually to ask God for forgiveness, clarity, strength, and endurance for myself. I focus on sending positive affirmations to both of my sons and share Scripture to encourage both of them to stay faithful, focused, and remember that they are not forgotten, but loved and protected.

I love both of my boys so much. They are both such different people. We all have a journey. I believe our job as parents here on this earth is to show our children encouragement, love, protection and give them positive affirmations to help them feel secure in their own bodies so that they can go out in the world and make a difference in their lives to share their own stories, what they have learned, help others and stay in their own truth.

I believe it is important for them to find their own tribe that helps them to let go of any negative energy and allow themselves to stay in the current moment.

We all struggle with not living in the current moment. I have had issues with looking back or experiencing anxiety about what will happen in the future. If we show our kids that right now, we love them, they will carry this with them.

I enjoy writing letters and cards for my boys to keep when I have moved on from this planet. I like showing my boys affection, telling them I love them, and sharing some of my Bible study and Scriptures that I have learned from. It is so important to trust God that he has our children in his hands, we can only guide them and show them the way, but it is ultimately their own choices.

We need to stay in the space of positive energy and exude this attitude in the presence of our children and others. The more we trust and remove anxiety, the more we can give the gift of love to others. Children are a gift from God and I believe it is so important to realize this fact and use the opportunity that we have during our parenting to affirm them, love them, accept them, give them the guidance that we know how, and continue to pray for them in their own journey of life here in earth school.

# SIX

# Health Struggles

Inner peace is the key during times of trials and tribulations. I work in a stressful environment that is fast-paced and constant. It is up to me to take the time and create the quietness that I need in order to listen to God. It does not come naturally for me to disengage and be quiet. I have had to teach myself with the help of meditation, breath work, prayer, and being alone purposefully. I have spent the majority of my time on this earth seeking stimulation that has not always been positive or helpful to me to move in the right direction towards inner peace. The blessing of moving back to the ocean and making the time to walk on the beach with no electronics and listening to the serene sound of the waves helps me to disconnect from society and stress.

I pray continuously to find the right food plan. I have the ability to attend yoga classes, play tennis, and work out at the gym several times per week. It is a constant battle, but I know stress affects the chemistry of our body as well. Meditation and relaxation are a key part of my life, and always will be. I have to set an alarm on my phone to remind myself to take five deep breaths several times per day in order to keep balance in my life and mindfulness to help me have cognizance of each moment being a gift from God to live and experience life in a positive mindset.

In respect to health, I have worked all my life to address the autoimmune disorders I have been diagnosed with. Celiac disease, hypothyroidism, fibromyalgia, diverticulitis, esophagitis, gastritis along with hypoglycemia and in February of 2022 they found two growths in my liver after several CT Scans due to abdominal pain, UTIs and kidney infections. At this time of my life, I endured a great deal of pain, hospital visits, uncertainty, multiple doctor visits and a medical leave from my work to take the time to obtain an accurate diagnosis. Liver disease and autoimmune was the main concern with the doctors. I had multiple GI tests that showed the various irritable bowel issues, but no cancer in the liver or the colon. Praise the Lord! I do believe the message from the Lord at this time of my life with the issue with my liver, was a sign from Him telling me to completely alleviate drinking alcohol. I have been a social drinker since high school and with both of my parents being alcoholics, I needed to stop consuming alcohol

I sought out guidance from my spiritual counselor, Jayne during this time off for medical leave to try to obtain answers and possible direction on next steps for my life and healing. Jayne and I had a few sessions and she had received word from the Lord that I was to be a Tribal Dancer. The meaning of this title is to, "Let go, say yes to life!". The consultation that I received from Jayne was that I need to be daring and dance to my heart's desire. I needed to unfurl my wings and fly. It will be important to cast aside the restrictions I place on myself in my workaholism addiction. I need to tune into the rhythm of my life. Laugh, Explore, and go beyond my predictable behavior. I tend to be a conservation person, not wanting to take risks as I have a fear of hurting myself physically.

I am skeptical about taking risks in daring sports. My life has been messy and chaotic, and that has been okay, but I need to learn to leave the dishes, run outside in the sprinklers and let go of being inhibited. It is okay to be vulnerable with yourself.

I have continued to want to meet the expectations of others and myself. Some of these expectations have been unrealistic. People have told me I'm "wound tight" and need to just relax and let things happen. I want to explore, expand and step into my extraordinary self. I have the desire to joyously fling my arms up to the heavens and dance. I believe with all of my health challenges, the Lord is teaching me to choose life on my terms. I need to clear out the mental and emotional clutter and move beyond situations I have outgrown. I have placed stringent rules on myself to be productive and not just accept each challenge as another opportunity to learn a new lesson. I need to learn to listen to the rhythm of my heart and follow my dreams.

A tribal dancer will turn on the music and move. It is not about looking good. It's about feeling the best inside our heart and expressing this is our own body and emotions. We need to express ourselves. Let go of any inhibitions or past guilt, shame or anger that we are hoarding in our bodies. I am a free spirit in nature, and do not like to be pinned down anywhere. If I allow myself to break free of these bindings that I instill upon myself, I can live a free life and it will transform into a healthy human being, in mind, body and spirit.

It has been difficult to eat the right food, keep my blood sugar balanced, and monitor my thyroid. I struggle with constant fatigue, brain fog, and joint pain.

My autoimmune diseases, and digestive issues have been difficult to endure. I have visited the ER more than ten times enduring excruciating abdominal pain and been sent away being told it is just "IBS". I have had my gallbladder removed and now experience more digestive issues since this particular surgery.

My confidence in the medical industry has diminished due to many tests and specialists with no answers. My stomach bloats out, appearing to be six months pregnant frequently, with no consistency in what type of food I am digesting. It has been difficult to stay positive and hopeful that a diagnosis will be found to help me with the abdominal pain, diarrhea nausea, and extreme fatigue I have had most all of my life. I am not a hypochondriac, and know that there must be an answer. I believe western medicine has some good explanations, but I also have spent thousands of dollars on holistic healing as well.

God is the only one that has the answer to our questions. (Exodus 23:25) Serve the Lord and healing will be yours. Worship the Lord your God, and his blessing will be on your food and water. I will take away sickness from you.

In Holy Yoga practice, I close my eyes and envision a white light coming through my skull and swirling through my intestines and around my liver healed. I had a healing session with Dana where she told me to envision a needle and thread sewing up the diverticulosis in my large intestine that was found after I was hospitalized a week with a small bowel instruction.

I have taught myself how to stop myself from negative self-talk and instead envision white light moving throughout my body healing my arthritic pain, digestive issues, bladder issues, female problems and inflammation. It is so important to connect with yourself internally and pay attention to what is really going on inside. We need to learn how to rest.

We all have the ability to self-heal. I truly believe that body symbology is real. Since I have been diagnosed with celiac disease, there is no consistency as to how I can react to food. I find that coffee and alcohol can cause pain in my joints and issues with my digestive system. I have met with several dietitians, holistic healers, and internal medicine doctors to try to obtain assistance with internal healing. I was given over fourteen supplements, a strict diet removing all dairy, gluten and sugar for six months. I felt better during this time, but it did not alleviate the bloating and pain that I was experiencing. I believe many of the holistics doctors are interested in a cure, but also can have a motive to sell their own supplements, and this is very expensive.

I believe herbs and supplements can be a good source of healing, but I believe it can be art in a seated position taking deep long breaths and instructing my students to picture themselves in a peaceful place, breathing deeply, releasing any negative thoughts and forgetting about the negative experiences that they had during the day.

I had one test called the HIDA scan, a test for the functionality of the gallbladder, which showed mine was only operating at 17 percent capacity, so I agreed to the surgery to remove my gallbladder. I probably did not need the surgery. After the surgery, it was a quick recovery, but painful, and I still continued to have abdominal pain.

In 2009, I had sought out multiple doctors questioning why I was constantly experiencing pain, diarrhea, dizziness, and bloating. After over forty years of my life, my endocrinologist ordered a blood test for celiac disease, which was positive. I finally had an explanation of over forty years of severe pain and discomfort. It was at that time that I tried many different consultations with dietitians, internal medicine doctors, and holistic advisors to try to find a diet that would work for me to alleviate the discomfort.

I have removed gluten and soy from my diet, and still experienced diarrhea and sleeplessness. I read a book called *Grain Brain*. This book was written to help explain how eating gluten and grains will cause brain fog and discomfort. I believe I have held shame, guilt and anger within my body and for many years and without using the breathwork and spiritual healing, would have remained sick the remainder of my life.

I believe we are what we eat, and it is all about finding the right balance for your own chemistry in your body.

When a person is diagnosed with celiac disease, there is still cross-contamination in the foods, the oils, and seasoning that restaurants use that cause side effects. It is hard to know what is safe to eat. I cannot juice or drink shakes or smoothies, as they make me sick.

On July 30, 2019, I developed a high-grade small intestinal bowel obstruction. I went to dinner with some friends and felt cramps shortly after eating.

The cramping progressively got worse. I was soaking wet, trying to go to the bathroom, and ended up passing out from the pain. I woke up leaning on the wall sitting on my toilet, very dizzy, and knew something was seriously wrong.

I had already endured over ten abdominal surgeries, multiple ER visits with IBS attacks and a gallbladder removal, but this was different.

My son took me to the ER and they immediately did a CAT scan that showed an obstruction in my small bowel. One of the prayer warriors in my life, my special friend Kim, came to visit with me and stay until I would fall asleep and pray that I would not have to endure another surgery. The doctors ordered a barium X-ray and saw that the obstruction had passed. It was a miracle. I was hospitalized for four days. The question is, what caused it? What was the message from God to me during this hospitalization and infection? (Jeremiah 30:17) God will restore your health. But I will restore you to health and heal your wounds, declares the Lord, because you are called an outcast, Zion for whom no one cares.

Upon return from the hospital, I researched "spiritual causes that lead to bowel disorders and digestive problems." A few items were revealed to me in prayer and meditation.

Here are a few items that made sense to me that could be contributing to my digestive issues:

1.  Inability to accept a situation or a person (my latest ex-husband!)
2.  Resentment
3.  The fear of letting go of old misconceptions

I truly believe God speaks to us during the times we are experiencing difficult circumstances, challenges, making the wrong life choices, and having bad attitudes. God reveals to us what needs to be worked on in our lives. It is in his timing to reveal what the message may be; like Job. He was stripped of everything, and tempted to sway from his faith. I refuse to blame God when things go wrong. I'm on a path to figure out how I can contribute by sharing my stories and identify the proper cause and effect of why things happen to us. It does nothing to stay dwelling on the pain and negativity.

I was so fortunate to not have to endure surgery during the small bowel obstruction hospitalization. Although the actual cause was not clear, I know that all the scar tissue from all other surgeries was an issue for my intestines. I needed to make the commitment to not drink any alcohol or coffee and only eat small meals several times a day due to my medical condition. This takes discipline, and I do not always follow this regimen.

I believe if we take the time to study more about eating healthy and consult with a dietician in respect to learning more about our digestive system, it will give us a better understanding of how we can be healthy and make better choices of what we eat and drink to nourish our bodies. I recommend the book, *Eat right 4 Your Blood Type* by Dr. Peter J D'Adamo.

The various hospitalizations that I have endured have given me an opportunity to reflect, stop my daily routine, and stop and listen to God.

All the pain I have endured in my body gives me the gratitude that I am still able to walk, exercise, eat, use the regular restroom, and the fact that I was gifted with birthing two healthy boys.

My health challenges and raising two sons have taught me about how people can use different methods of handling their emotional issues that are not healthy for their bodies. My parents chose alcohol, cigarettes, and marijuana to avoid addressing their own issues, and I suffered the repercussions of being raised by broken people that were trying to do their best in parenting me.

Life is not easy. Stress management has always been a challenge for me. I thank God for all of the strength he has provided me during my lifetime. There is goodness in every circumstance if we stop to listen, it's just taking the time to calm down and stop. Lord, help us all to discern what time to stop, breathe, and listen.

There is always a positive. I'm not discounting the excruciating pain I have endured, but I know that there is another side after we experience pain and a purpose and message from God during these challenging times. I believe in body symbology, and the intestines/ digestive system is a direct correlation to emotions. Our bodies are always a work in process.

# SEVEN

# Symbols And Messages

I am particularly interested in symbols and messages from God to teach me what my purpose should be here on planet Earth. God has given me the gift of motivation, but I need to use it for his benefit, not my own. He has blessed me with children, and it is hard to work with them when they do not process information the same as me. I have trouble relating to them sometimes knowing that my tone needs to be encouraging, non-judgmental and soft. I struggle with my direct approach with people and they can misinterpret me to be insensitive. I plan to work on this in myself this coming year and the rest of my life.

Lord, help me to see and hear what I look like and sound like to others. I want to personify that "gentle and quiet spirit" that you desire for me to be a vessel for you, showing grace towards others as Jesus Christ did for us during his time here on earth (Proverbs 15:18). Hot tempers start fights; a calm, cool spirit keeps the peace.

In 2019, I had a symbol shown to me through a friend of mine as we were coming back from Big Bear, California, after a quick getaway trip. There was a sick, starving coyote that crossed our path on the road. You typically do not see coyotes by themselves in plain view approaching your car and stopping. His eyes were scary. According to Worldbirds of Nature, September 24, 2021, the symbolism of the coyote remains enigmatic, being both a trickster yet also a teacher. Coyote energy is a sign of trouble or good fortune. The Coyote is a wild sage whose message comes indirectly.

The coyote is not a candid spirit, but one that often resorts to chicanery and jokes to get a point across. The Coyote spirit animal is strikingly paradoxical and usually hard to categorize. The coyote is a teacher of hidden wisdom with a sense of humor, so the message may be that of a joke. I believe the message is don't be tricked by foolish appearances. The spirit of the coyote may remind us to not take things too seriously and bring more balance between wisdom and playfulness.

The wisdom delivered by the coyote spirit animal is rarely direct. The way of the coyote is to teach through ways that do not appear straightforward. It may also use subterfuge or trickery to reach its goal or deliver its message. I am generally straightforward in all of my communication, both at my workplace and in personal relationships. Perhaps this message for me was to stop and take a different approach with work colleagues and get my point across more "delicately."

The most interesting part of this symbol of the coyote that appeared to me is that at this time of my life, I was struggling with taking work too seriously and not putting balance into my position at my work.

I have struggled with people not working at my speed and with the level of intensity that I have for my work. I can come across as demanding, impatient, rude, and curt. I do not want to be personified as the "mean" person who drives everyone crazy. I want to be a resource, and someone that is helpful and encouraging.

I have had a tendency to take things too seriously and not make my position at work "playful." Adaptability is key in my position. I pray that I can learn to adapt to the environment I am working in and be an asset to the company I represent.

Another example of a message that I have received from God is when I had a massage from a therapist in Texas. I have massages once a month, and I believe I have encountered visits from the Holy Spirit during these healing experiences. My massage therapist in Texas had my mother and Biff both appear to her during my massage and give her the message that I was going to be okay and that they were in my presence. I see a massage therapist in California and she has also given me some distinct messages that I believe to be from the Holy Spirit through angels.

My massage therapist in California, who had given me a massage before a Christmas party for my work, stated that she had a good feeling for my upcoming career opportunity. I thought it was interesting, considering there were some changes happening with the company that I was presenting at the time. I put this revelation and message aside.

One month thereafter, this therapist stated that during the massage she had a vision of a bamboo fence and someone was holding a camera above the fence. She asked me if anyone was watching me that I knew of. I had to try to process this; I was uncertain as to who might be "watching me".

I asked my therapist, was this a good feeling in your vision? She stated, "Absolutely!" I still had a fear that something was not right. Ironically enough, I prayed about this and asked the Lord for clarification and a clearer message from this vision that was shared with me.

That same evening I was reading my book *The Power of Your Attitude* by Stan Toler and there was a specific section on the bamboo plant.

In Toler's book, the bamboo plant pertains to principles of positive thinking in our lives. Positive thinking cannot dwell in past or future circumstances. The book then mentioned the bamboo plant being a lesson. It is technically considered a species of grass, but is one of the strongest natural materials and is prized as a building material in certain parts of the world. It has a higher compressive strength than wood, brick, or concrete, and its tensile strength is nearly as great as steel.

In order to build a forest of bamboo plants, it takes perseverance. It grows deep before it grows tall. The interesting thing about my massage therapist's vision is she specifically stated this was a short bamboo plant.

For many months or even years after planting, there's no visible growth of the bamboo plant.

While the plant is gaining strength below the surface, the bamboo farmer must wait patiently, trusting that the hardy plant will eventually emerge from the ground. There is nothing to do but wait. It's a lesson in perseverance. What a revelation for me to learn about the symbology of a bamboo plant and the inner strength and growth!

I believe this was a symbol for me to address my past as part of my plantation of bamboo. Perseverance and faith in Christ is why I still have the ability to continue to keep going when things have been difficult in my life circumstances.

I have learned so much from Jayne Clark, who is a spiritual coach. Jayne also believes that Jesus is the son of God, has the Holy Spirit in her life, and has been given the gift of being a seer.

Jayne teaches about nature's healing and the shaman's teachings, which is intriguing to me. I have Native American ancestry from both my mother's and father's side of the family. My grandfather was 99 percent Cherokee. My parents were particularly interested in the Native Americans and the spiritual teachings from them.

Jayne did a series on the medicine wheel that the shamans taught in regards to the earth elements, spiritual animals for healing, and the meaning of the EAST/WEST/NORTH/SOUTH directions and how they correlate to balancing our lives. Jayne studied under Alberto Villoldo and the Four Winds Society to learn about the medicine wheel.

Here is a brief synopsis of the teaching by Jayne. I would highly recommend her as a counselor and spiritual coach for anyone who has suffered greatly from relational issues and is trying to find peace within themselves, particularly in nature.

The teaching of the medicine wheel represents balance and manifesting what is available to us. We need to check in with what is in balance.

Fire, water, air, and earth are the elements that can help us achieve overall wellness in our emotional, physical, spiritual, and inner selves. It can open our positive energy up to others when we become more sensitive to these symbols.

We create a sacred space and passageway into the spiritual world.

The northern direction represents our soul. It incorporates the element earth and the spiritual animal of the hummingbird. We have different gifts and talents, and even if we have the same talents, each person can express them differently. This is how God made us as human beings with souls. The soul houses our contracts and lessons to be learned here in Earth School, what we came here to fulfill; we need to learn our purpose.

The medicine that the hummingbird represents is our path from fear to love. The hummingbird represents grounding. The hummingbird can flap its wings vigorously, but still remain calm and still. We need to remain grounded and make an impact on the world. The hummingbird represents the miracle of life showing us love and happiness. This spiritual teacher finds the sweetness of life. We need to train ourselves to see the beauty in the ugly. We learn to see ourselves and appreciate the beauty within us and our surroundings. We need to use our intuition and open up our path in each present moment to demonstrate what is in our heart, not focus on the outward.

We have come to this planet to grow, not remain stagnant in negativity seeing the ugliness of this world.

The Mayans believed the south direction correlated with fire. The south represents the physical body. It teaches us balance for finances, survival needs, and flight/fight when you face the south.

The direction of the west relates to the jaguar spiritual animal. The jaguar is the medicine for emotional healing. In the jungle, the jaguar has no predators. He is at the top of the environment and sees clearly in the dark. The jaguar is known for his eyesight. He is known as the "ruler of the underworld." He can see into the ugliness and can kill in one blow.

He has aggressive energy when dealing with fears and insecurities. When we call upon our medicine of the jaguar, we call to devour our fears. The jaguar is patient and waits before pouncing prematurely for his prey. We need to hunt for patience. He tracks and follows.

We need to move in life fearlessly, look where our roots originate and heal ourselves from negativity. We can devour our fears and grow and evolve in the most unlikely of places and circumstances. We need to learn healing from the jaguar and receive this power, embody aggressiveness and receive the warning of danger.

The Egyptians used the felines as a passageway to track and tap into their own psyche. We have free will and choice, and we can select a different destiny. Our consciousness can go anywhere, but we must stop and listen to the lessons and use this planet Earth in this existence to help us live prosperous and healthy lives

Water is the element that correlates to the emotional aspect of our being. We use water to clean, cook, wash, and it grows our food. Nature needs it. The value of our ocean is the salt water. It cleans and is a purifying substance that cleanses the energetic field.

Water is the representation of the spirit. It is feminine and becomes fluid with life. When things come up, we can call upon the direction of the west. When we face the west, we can ask for the water to wash away our restrictions of mental fatigue and allow openness to envelop our being. This gives us the fluidity to release the negative energy we experience when feeling fatigued and frustrated in life. In nature, fog burns off, as does the fear when we seek this healing. We need to be in the consciousness of light and love. If we have a greater faith in the Holy Spirit, we are in a better position to receive this healing.

The spiritual animal of the east is the eagle, which represents our spirit. The element is air. Our thoughts, creativity, and expressions of truth and perceptions are part of us that have incarnated into the high self—the Holy Spirit. This is the heavenly realm that is eliminating separation from us as humans.

We are in communion with the angels, timeless, eternal and infinite, the luminous body, the light body. When passing from this world, we go back to this stage. We are everywhere in a spiritual existence.

The eagle soars above the storms of life and we call upon this spiritual animal as a medicine to remove evil. We can see above. The eagle's eyes allow us to see the details and hidden truths of spirits in the upper world. This brings a perfect balance of heaven and earth. The eagle's beak is connected to its jaw and is designed to crush. We need to be careful with the words we speak. It has a vibration of uplifting truth. We need to speak of love and compassion.

The eagles glide effortlessly. We need to bless our minds and ask the Holy Spirit to guide us.

Stress comes from what we are making up. We need to focus on what is happening now.

East is the direction of the rising sun. It gives us opportunities to start over. We make mistakes in relationships. We need to offer ourselves compassion, see the deepest wounds, and not take things so personally.

The medicine wheel represents the circle of life. We have repeated patterns that we need to shed at a deeper level for renewal of our life. We are not to go backwards in life, but to learn lessons from each pattern and move forward in a positive manner. The feeling of being constricted is not healthy.

Staying at a job that is not fulfilling, in a relationship that is destructive, is not good for us. We need to own our personal power and as the serpents shed the belly, this can soften our lower back pain.

When we do not feel supported in our lives, we need to make room to embody our physical being. Many people can go out of their bodies and try to escape reality. We need to stay grounded.

We need to track our fears and do this with consciousness. We learn our lessons and how to let go when we get to the core of our being and experience this soul retrieval. When we have fears of lack, we can release this fear and let it go. The thing is never the "thing"; we need to go deep into our spirit. We ARE light and love. We are free!

There is another spiritual animal which is the serpent for medicine. When we need to deal with our physical existence, the serpents teach us to shed and renew ourselves. The snakes start shedding at their eyes first, so they can SEE more clearly. The head represents our mental fatigue. The ears and the brain coincide with our solar plexus chakra, representing our truth.

I believe the seven chakras teach us the energies of our bodies. There is scientific evidence that we are energetic beings. According to the Scientific Basis of Integrative Medicine (NCBI), the chakras are the main energy centers of the body. When the chakras are open and are flowing freely, energy can run through them and harmony exists between the physical body, mind and spirit.

According to www.healthline.com, our chakras refer to the various energy centers of our body that correspond to specific nerve bundles and internal organs. The seven major chakras run from the base of our spine to the top of our head. If the energies are blocked, we may experience physical and emotional symptoms related to a particular chakra.

I believe the chakras give us an understanding of our spiritual and energetic parts of our human bodies. When I meditate and pray, I envision each chakra and start at the crown chakra.

I see the light (for me, this is the Holy Spirit) coming into my body from the top of my skull and it moves throughout each chakra. Each chakra has a purpose for our flesh and spirit.

The medicine wheel can be applied in relationships, health, job/career, and finances. Jayne gives us an analogy of being a weeder or a gardener.

The weeder always looks for the cleaning—this is like the serpent and jaguar. The gardener continues to plant and heal—this is like our hummingbirds and eagles. We need to work at being gardeners here in this Earth School and not weeders. We need to move on and learn from the lessons that are taught to us from our elements, spiritual animals, and directions. If we stay in the realm of planting and healing, we can find beauty in the world.

We should use our individual strengths, attributes, talents, etc., to the best of our ability while we are here...not necessarily for superficial gain, but just simply for growth, expansion, and sharing.

We were given these talents and attributes for a reason. (1 Corin 12:4-11) all spiritual gifts come from the same spirit, our Lord.

We need to use them. We all, as individuals, have things about us that add to the whole picture of life. We owe it to ourselves then to help ourselves expand in all ways, just as much as we are able to help others expand themselves in all ways.

So that core self, the underlying, at peace, meditational, unconditionally loving self, the spiritual self that knows it doesn't have to do, be, think, or feel anything specific in order to be whole, worthy, loving, and lovable, is your underlying base and through-line of your life. Just like for everybody else's lives. We are all one. We are all worthy.

We are all infinite and beautiful. And then, in addition, we are all ego-conscious beings who are a balance of dark and light, with our own individuality, and need to find our ultimate balance within that and keep evolving and growing.

I would never say it is narcissistic to want to use your personal attributes to the best of your ability. What becomes narcissistic or toxic is when you misuse them instead. It becomes a necessary question of why you are wanting to do what you are doing. If what is behind it is actually stemming from a feeling of lack or need in any way, then what you are doing becomes self-serving. That is the difference.

I truly understand God's light. I have seen it, felt it, dreamt it, and know it. Jesus was described as the Light of this world and without him living inside of me, I would not have the capability of having the peace that I do within myself.

I still struggle in human flesh on a daily basis, but forgive myself and ask for forgiveness. God gets me, and he gets you too. We all have one heart, a purpose and a story.

I am intrigued by the Holy Spirit working through dreams. I have just been given the book by James W. and Michal Ann Goll entitled *The Prophetic Power Of Dreams, Revelations, and the Spirit of Wisdom: Dream Language.* God speaks to us through our unconscious state, as that is when we stop and listen. Life gets so busy with "stuff" and we forget to stop and listen, and I have been guilty of this my whole life. Trying to stay busy and being productive at all times does not give us an opportunity to listen to what God is saying. Our Holy Spirit strives to speak to us and we need to make ourselves available.

I have been seeing a spiritual coach for over four years, Dana Patterson of *Spiritual Homework*, that has given me the knowledge and understanding of the fact that all power and control is in the moment. It is so important for us to understand our triggers from our past hurts. Dana has taught me to learn how to clear my old patterns of becoming bitter and angry with people who I feel are deliberately hurting me, ignoring me and causing me to feel rejected and thought of as a nuisance. My upbringing had betrayal, and I was surrounded by a challenging vibrational frequency.

I have struggled in relationships due to my past belief that I was not accepted. My parents did not pay much attention to me as an only child and they were much older when they conceived me. I was told to "play with my Barbies" and go away.

I would cry and ask for attention in an annoying manner, becoming boisterous, and had deep emotional wounds from not feeling seen. I would strive so hard to get my mom's attention and when family or others would come around, they would tell me I was a spoiled brat and annoying and too loud.

I continued to have this belief that I needed to seek out attention by going out of my way to be seen. This original part of childhood caused me to have deep emotional pain and due to the trauma and loss, my energy was unbalanced and I continued to seek out the wrong friends and attention from men.

If we are still living on this planet, we have work to do. There are miracles that can happen. We attract what we are; our vibrational frequency can change into a positive surrounding for us. Life is happening through us.

We must control what we are attracting. It takes deep, lifelong work to realize what you are bringing in and paying attention to the frequency that you are creating. The road we pick is what we will manifest. We all have our own core belief system and we need to have clarity as to our self-worth and our vibration needs to continue to rise.

A good way to raise your vibration is using deep breathing, focusing on being in a positive mindset no matter what you are enduring, and envisioning you loving yourself. I close my eyes and envision something pleasing to my eyes or smelling something that I particularly enjoy. The ocean typically comes to my mind immediately and I envision myself breathing in the ocean air and listening to the waves in a relaxed state of mind.

I also picture my late husband kissing me and holding me as he did. I felt safe and secure and loved. We need to make sure that we are respecting ourselves at all times and giving grace when you are struggling with negativity. I have studied dreams and read the book *Dream Language* by James W. and Michal Ann Goll. This is a Christian-based book on how our Holy Spirit speaks to us in our dream state. I have had dreams that I will remember all of my life. The Lord has always spoken to me through my dreams. I have mentioned a few of these dreams here in this text to give you examples of what I believe are messages from God to help give me direction for my life.

I write each dream in a book next to my bed. I believe it is important to pray and take the time to discern what the messages and meaning of your dreams can be for you. I share my dreams with other friends in order to obtain their assessment and possible explanation of what they think God's message might be for me. I have one particular friend that has some incredible dreams that she has shared with me, and we discuss together what we believe our messages from the Lord are for guidance on how we are to work through our challenges and stay positive about our future.

I believe the Lord can also speak to us through symbols and gifts that are given to us with specific meaning. I was given a Christmas ornament from a dear friend, Denise, who was my women's Bible study leader when I was pregnant with my second son. Denise gave me this Christmas ornament called "The Prophet." I did not understand why she would think I was a prophet.

The Lord has spoken to me since I was a young child and I have discounted the fact that he has chosen me to be a woman to show others how he works through his Holy Spirit. I speak boldly about my faith in Jesus Christ. It is important to understand the gifts you are blessed with and be grateful.

The book *Dream Language* speaks about how some people are prophetically gifted and receive primarily external dreams rather than internal. This book spoke volumes to me. God has given me many internal dreams of self-disclosure to cleanse. If our gifts consist of prophetic ministry, they are highly revelatory in nature. I dream about nature all the time.

We need to understand what we are creating. We all have the creative ability to connect with ourselves, but we must listen to our inner voice and truly understand our triggers. I realize prayer can be difficult for many of us, as we cannot see who we are praying to, but I particularly love the verse (II Corin 5:7) For we walk by faith, not by sight. When I say this scripture, it gives me the perspective that I must always have the belief that no matter where I am or who I am with, I always have the ability to pray to God. He never leaves us or forsakes us.

# EIGHT

# Church Life And Scripture Teachings

Women's Bible studies have helped me to connect with other women who have also experienced loss, suffering, and the feelings of helplessness and failure. We are all women of flesh living in this fallen world trying to make a difference and for some women, to procreate offspring who will contribute to this world in a positive manner. When we witness our child hurting, it is so hard to know what next steps to take. I have spent many nights on my knees, walking on the beach, speaking in my tongues, and crying out to the Lord asking for strength and understanding. I just keep hearing, *"Let go, let me take care of this for you, Serena."*

The Type "A" personality that I have, it is a constant struggle to abide by the Lord's command to release control. The stories of Paul, Jesus, Job, and several other biblical characters show they endured so much pain and confusion in the fallen world, but continued to remain steadfast in their faith. I aspire to also have the ability to do so in trials and tribulations for the remainder of my time here on earth. I have never deviated from my faith, blamed God, or been angry with Him. My gift has been my faith in God. This has been a positive character trait that God has blessed me with in this lifetime.

I attended church at Capo Beach Church in San Juan Capistrano for a number of years and heard one of the most profound sermons that really hit home.

This particular message was based on (John 1:1–7). The message states that life did not exist without God and we do not exist without God. We as humans came into existence due to the word of God.

Jesus exists with us at all times. He doesn't love us more when we are singing verses than when we are worshiping. He remains consistent in his love for us at all times. Without him, we would not exist, as he is God in living form. He is constantly in our presence. Every person entering life, he brings into light. He was in the world, the world was there through him, and yet the world did not even notice him. It is up to us to bring the light to those around us. We that have chosen to believe in Jesus Christ as the Son of God, sent to this earth to bring us salvation, forgiveness and eternal life, are taught that life has purpose. If we believe in the teachings of Jesus Christ and the Scriptures, the fact that Jesus Christ is God in human form, we are taught that we are ultimately responsible to be disciples to show the light that exists within us that are living with and in him.

Jesus hasn't gone anywhere; he exists in spirit form and we are taught that his Holy Spirit resides inside of us if we choose to have this belief of the purpose of life.

One of the most profound meanings of life to me is to learn how to live in the moment. If our thoughts are focused on the past, then we are not living in the moment where God is.

If our thoughts are focused on the future, then we are not living with God where he is NOW. This is so important for us to understand.

It is difficult to actually live in every moment. We spend time worrying about what might happen in the future, or focusing on regrets from our past, which is counterproductive to what God wants us to focus on. This is taking us away from living where we exist now.

Have you ever noticed that things often get worse when you commit yourself to fasting and prayer? The devil does not want us to seek ways to serve the Lord, but his agenda is for us to be self-serving. When we are practicing ways to serve the Lord, we will be attacked. Jesus was attacked in the desert and tempted by the devil when he was hungry and thirsty after spending 40 days in the wilderness.

My home church is now The Orchard in Temecula, CA. Pastor Jim Jackson is authentic, entertaining, direct, and loves the Lord with all his heart. He has a way of sharing the scriptures that are relatable to many people. He speaks in series to include several topics such as dealing with abandonment. The Lord built us to live in community. We are built to do life together. I believe that when I share about my personal experiences in regards to suffering from the loss of several loved ones, my health struggles, witnessing my loved ones that have their own struggles, in addition to work challenges, it may help others in the community who can relate to me and potentially give them similar tools to know how to most past the hurt and welcome the pain identifying the purpose in it.

Pastor Jim stated in one of our sermons that some choose opportunities they believe are right or godly, but leave chaos or destroy relationships, leaving emotional damage.

Abandoning God-given situations is evidence of selfishness and spiritual immaturity. Relational separation and abandonment are a reality. We must not let someone else's behavior dictate our view of ourselves or our value to God. (Matthew 28:20) God will never leave or forsake us.

It is so important when you are spending the time to look within, pray, and know that you are protected, loved and if we stay committed to servicing the Lord, we will be rewarded if not in this lifetime, in eternity. The bible mentions rewards that await the believer who serves the Lord faithfully in this world (Matthew 10:41). A great reward is promised to those who are persecuted for Jesus' sake. Various crowns are mentioned in (2 Timothy 4:8). Finally, there is laid up for me the crown of righteousness, which the Lord, the righteous Judge, will give to me on that Day, and not to me only but also to all who have loved His appearance.

When we draw attention to the effectiveness of a prayer priority, it can give us clarity as to our purpose and meaning of enduring trials and tribulations we experience. Your adversary, the devil, is especially content with a lukewarm variety of Christianity. The devil has discovered that prayerless churches and prayerless Christians do him no harm.

In fact, the prayerless church does much to foster an environment in which the great deceiver can work his dark arts. Godly people give their best to godly relationships. (I Thess. 5:16-18).

We are to be faithful to pray for others to be faithful; then tell them we are faithfully praying for them to be faithful. Pastor Jim teaches us how prayer can mold the heart of people and move the hand of God.

In times of difficulty, we must not give up, but stand up! I love that song by Elton John, "I'm Still Standing!".

When we pray, we should not be surprised by increased troubles. James says that we are to resist. Resistance is offered in the face of attack. In times of leisure and rest, no resistance is required. When troubles are greatly increased, anchor deep in the word of God and hold on. It won't be long before a victory is won.

Immature Christians make the grave error of thinking that their trial is evidence that they are doing something wrong, when in fact that very trial is evidence that they are doing something right! Keep holding out, even when it seems that your prayers are stirring up more trouble.

Satan wants us to believe that he is inexhaustible, when in truth, he suffers a crippling lack of endurance. Satan has no power unless it is given to him. He was removed from heaven as a fallen angel that chose to leave God's kingdom and discover his own "power." We as human beings have the ability to not allow him to be given any power over our lives or let him influence our thinking.

Church life has given me an opportunity to fellowship with others who also believe that Jesus is the son of God.

The attendance of church has given me the opportunity to volunteer, help others, share in my faith, and enjoy worship music. I enjoy learning about the biblical scriptures and how they pertain to my life here on earth living for a purpose.

Our legacy will have a lot to do with the depth of our belief in our Christ given identity. When we spend time in community with others who believe the same as we do, it will help us influence others and be an example that God has created us to be. We learn to speak from the heart.

# NINE

# Holy Yoga

God speaks to us through our bodies. He created seven chakras to teach us to balance and focus on the "shell" that God has created for us to exist on this planet and a soul that lives inside of our earthly bodies. If we look within the body and really see balance and purpose, it gives us the ability to learn to love ourselves.

I started doing yoga in the 1990s to get exercise. There are so many types of yoga. I have tried Bikram (hot yoga), and this particular practice gave me such a blessing of feeling cleansed inside and out. It is hard work, but very healing. All yoga practice has helped me to look within myself and focus on all of the chakras within my body.

Yoga is a tool I use to help heal from trauma. For many believers in Christ, they hear the word yoga or chakras and are immediately turned off with the belief that it is not of Christ and should be avoided. In the practice of Holy Yoga, we incorporate the Holy Spirit and bring Him into our being and only focus on Christ within us. I have had discussions with many christian people that do not believe the practice of yoga can be incorporated with the belief in Jesus Christ. As christians, the spirit of God comes upon us through the Holy Spirit and while i am practicing Holy Yoga, he gives me the words to share with my students to bring peace and joy into their soul by appreciating their bodies and organs that they are gifted with in their human body that was created by God.

It is our assignment from God to share about the resurrection of Jesus Christ as the son of God and teach about the gospel. Holy Yoga is a tool for me to share about my faith.

I have enjoyed restoration, hatha, and vinyasa yoga, which all incorporate movement and focus on our muscles, balance, and looking within. It helps you to remove yourself from thinking and focus on prayer and meditation. It helped me to remove the anxiety that I experience on a daily basis that I need to heal. I feel safe in my own body when I am healing and focused on the good inside of me.

In the practice of yoga, I see the Christ consciousness within me and actually envision a white light that He brings through my body throughout all of the chakras. I feel the Holy Spirit moving within my body, and also can feel the angels surrounding me during my practice. I am able to incorporate my spiritual belief in Christ within me as a believer; that he truly is the son of God and part of the Trinity of the Divine. I can actually see the Spirit within me.

Mind, body, and spirit have a whole new meaning to me now. I have always enjoyed working out and exercising in addition to prayer, meditation, and learning God's Word.

In Holy Yoga, we incorporate Scripture to the practice of healing our bodies during yoga. We incorporate Bible Scriptures and share how we find inner peace, calmness, and serenity, and share our love with others. We study a book called *Eat This Book* by Eugene H. Peterson. In it, Peterson states, "An interest in souls divorced from interest in Scriptures leaves us without a text that shapes our souls."

The definition of chakras is each center of spiritual power in the human body, usually considered to be seven in number. Chakras are various focal points used in a variety of ancient meditation practices. Chakra (cakra in Sanskrit) means "wheel" and refers to energy points in your body. They are thought to be spinning disks of energy that should stay "open" and aligned, as they correspond to bundles of nerves, major organs, and areas of our energetic body that affect our emotional and physical well being.

I believe it is important for us to have our energy running freely through our body and experiencing harmony between the physical body, mind and spirit. God created our bodies from the earth. The first verse in the bible, (Genesis 1:1) tells us that God has created everything, including all matter and energy. This means that God can't be identical to the universe, or can He be identical to any aspect of the universe. Since energy is a part of the created universe, we must conclude that God can't be energy. This is found in the Encyclopedia Britannica.

Christian meditation entails obedience in the next breath. An example is in the Book of Joshua: "This book of the Law shall not depart from your mouth, but you shall meditate on it day and night, so that you may be careful to do according to all that is written in it." Meditation can be considered not from God, but I believe that if we incorporate our belief in Jesus as the son of God and the biblical scriptures teaching us that we need to be content and have peace in the presence of God, we can use the practice of meditation to honor God and our bodies that He has created. (1 Peter 4:7) The end of all things is near. Therefore be clear minded and self-controlled so that you can pray.

In my Holy Yoga practice, I believe it gives me an opportunity to share about my faith and release control. I particularly enjoy during my practice envisioning the Holy Spirit coming into my body, speaking to me, and giving me the ability to stop my mind from wandering and staying focused on breathing and exercising in the exact moment.

I found an app on my phone for Christian meditation. It is called Abide. I am a believer in prayer and meditation, but it takes practice and knowing how to meditate. To have the ability to completely empty my mind of any thoughts and truly relax and go into the spiritual realm is a very challenging task for me. I believe that meditation needs to come from God. He created us with energy and energy chakras and we need to take that into consideration when meditating. I have had the blessed ability to see the white light move from the top of my head down to the bottom of my feet. I have felt that energy rush run throughout my body.

I like to listen to Scripture, soft music, and also work on the balances of my chakras to appreciate the body that God created for me to live in temporarily on this planet. It is so easy to get wrapped up in the flesh and what it can give us.

When we are acting in faith, this is the opposite of living with anxiety. We need to allow the feeling and the third eye (Christ center chakra) to gently gaze upon the word *faithful*. Envisioning each letter of faithfulness. Sound bowls. Inner-feelings of faithfulness consume all anxiety.

Be faithful to our truth, intuition, the God presence within us, love, our path that is unfolding, surrender, gently contemplate the feeling of being faithful to consume every cell, organ, tissue, ligament, tendon, all system of the body to be cleansed of all anxiety placed with faith. The physical and emotional body come together emerging with the inner feelings of the faithful.

When we are experiencing despair, we are not encountering pleasure in our life. The third eye allows awareness to softly gaze upon the word pleasurable. The positive spiritual energy of pleasure. Consume all feelings of pleasure vs. despair. Pleasure in work, relationships, in the home, and everything that is antagonistic to pleasure to dissolve and is released. The holy experience of Serena. The positive spiritual energy knowing that it is divine for us to bring positive spiritual energy into our entire life experience. Pleasure needs to permeate and consume all cells and body systems. The physical and emotional body becomes one and whole with pure positive energy. Let go of all negative feelings of despair and merge with pleasure.

The opposite of being remorseful is experiencing enjoyment in our lives. I have been unavailable to my sons due to work. The inner feelings of enjoyment need to consume all remorse. Pure and positive spiritual energy brings forth enjoyment in life. It is safe to enjoy my life, it is good to find enjoyment in relationships, work, and home. Our focus needs to be pure, positive and spiritual energy for our lives moving forward. Knowing the truth of who we are, we have the capability and authority to bring this into our lives.

All issues pertaining to remorse we know that our joy and freedom and divine expression goes forth through the pure energy we bring into our life.

All feelings of faithfulness, pleasure and enjoyment need to consume our emotions and physical body. We need to experience perfect calibration and peace. Our paths will unfold and we will gain insight and wisdom in all relationships and circumstances.

Life will be fulfilling if we can learn the expressions of love, imagination, joy, peace, serenity, sincerity, harmony, consistency, and faithfulness. When we learn how to encapsulate all of these gifts of the Holy spirit, our lives will be perfectly synthesized in every aspect of our own being. (Galatians 5:22-23) But the Holy Spirit produces this kind of fruit in our lives: love, joy, peace, patience, kindness, goodness, faithfulness, gentleness, and self control. There is no law against these things.

The outcome of living by these principles for our lives will be attributed to incorporating loyalty, truth, dedication, and having a healthy emotional and spiritual state of being. This will help us with intimacy, friendships, having compassion for others, being accurate and having the insight to make the right decisions for our lives.

# TEN

# Newfound Peace

I have had the opportunity to participate in several women's retreats and share my testimony. I enjoy watching the people in the audience resonate with my story and relate to the pain, but the main goal is to give them encouragement to keep the faith in knowing there is purpose in all of life's hurts and tribulations. When we stop and think about what Christ endured, our tragedies and hurts seem minimal. I can't imagine being nailed to a cross, beaten and ridiculed, and being innocent and taking it all for the purpose of saving souls, but that is exactly what Christ did for us. It seems selfish to dwell on what we have endured here on earth, knowing that Christ gave the ultimate sacrifice. When I am in self-pity mode, it helps me to remember Christ and his face kneeling and praying to the Lord on his last night, knowing what was to come for him.

I have had the pleasure of meeting with several leaders within the work environment and church functions. It has given me encouragement hearing other people's stories and how they encountered life's challenges and remained strong, uplifted, and encouraged, even during their own challenges in life. I had the pleasure of speaking on a panel of women at a Women's Workshop at our church held by Kimberley Loska, whom I work with in the Children's Ministry at my church. She was our keynote speaker for the "Untying the Ties that Bind" session.

Kimberly remains positive and faithful after her own experiences in life. It can be so hard to hear others' challenging stories, but also helpful to hear how other women look up to Christ to help them with their challenges. Kimberley states that in tragedy, there are three things you must do. 1). Look up. 2) Reach out. 3) Step forward.

We all have the obligation to contribute during this lifetime. I see my challenges now as being an opportunity, and not happening to me, but for me. Life is a gift. Christ gave us the assignment to be disciples, and I believe this is part of our duty to him to reach out to others and show them how our own faith has helped us endure loss, hurt, and pain.

I often spend time alone, thinking about what my real life's purpose is, and I reflect back on specific times when I was making the wrong decisions, choosing to spend time with the wrong people, when all I was lacking was true self-love. It can take a lifetime to find real self-love, and I have had the opportunity to spend time during prayer and spiritual retreats in reflecting back to the time when I was a little girl and did not know how to love myself. Many people put up walls to protect themselves against being hurt, when who they are really hurting is themselves, by not allowing themselves to look within and appreciate who they are and what goodness they can experience and appreciate within themselves.

I spent so many years of my life seeking love from outside of myself, when all along it was right within my own heart. It is hard to recognize that we are self-sabotaging ourselves by not accepting who we are and loving our own self first and foremost.

This is the true meaning of really being in love. We must love ourselves first, before we are capable of giving ourselves to others and falling in love with other human beings.

I have prayed to God my whole life, and can honestly say that many prayers have not been truly authentic in knowing what I was really asking for or thanking God for, by spending my prayer time in self-focus, not really looking deep within my own heart in knowing that God is in control of my life and already knows my future and the blessings that will be coming to me throughout my lifetime.

It is hard to comprehend the infiniteness of Christ and understand that he is all-knowing. We humans can be so shallow in focusing on the tangible, when in reality, it is about the spirit. We are souls living in human bodies. Life is temporary, and we must realize it is an opportunity to learn and love and give back to others. True love is hard to find, but we must find it within ourselves first and through our own spirit before we can give it to others.

Throughout my life, I have been involved in many women's Bible study groups and particularly appreciate the teachings of Beth Moore. She is authentic and knows the Scripture. I had an opportunity to attend the *Living Proof* Live conference in 2019 and learned a few steps from Beth's teachings from Acts 20 and 2 Timothy 4:16–18.

1. We have everything it takes to be the most compelling [insert your purpose here] on earth
2. In an effort to be culturally compelling, we have forfeited our uniqueness
3. We get to live a life worth dying for
4. We have a legacy of bold truth and bold tenderness
5. We are called to relationships that would be the envy of the world
6. We are recipients of prophetic insights, partial but plenty
7. Though we walk in harm's way, we shall make it safely home

Beth started the conference by asking the question, "What do you find the most compelling in a person? What makes it distinctive to you? What makes you scoot across the table closer to that person?" My answer to this was the following:

1. Honesty
2. Passion
3. Integrity
4. Loving
5. Kindness
6. Boldness
7. Compassion
8. Wisdom

Some other women in the group stated they found it to be humbly confident, transparent, and comfortable in their own skin.

"Compelling" is not the same thing as exciting; you want to find out what it is that drives that person. The definition in Webster is forceful and demanding attention and convincing. The spirit of God uses compelling people.

All it takes to be different in this world is not to be self-consumed. Life is temporary and we must stay focused and give our attention to what is eternal.

We think we will be more compelling if we just blend in with the world. Don't try to be "cooler." You need to be unique. People are fascinated by weirdness.

When we are operating the way God created us to, it pulls people toward us. People want to live for something so dear, they want to die for it. My life is a value to my Christ, not to myself. We all have a purpose for our life. We want to be relieved of self-preoccupation. It is the Holy Spirit who compels.

Our calling is discipleship. You can ask yourself, "What is my assignment in being a disciple that I was called to be in serving God here on earth"? It is important to understand our spiritual gifts and how God wants us to teach others about Him. When we get to heaven, all that will matter is that we bring people up (Acts 20:20). Do not hesitate to preach anything that is helpful. Don't talk about what you want to talk about.

We can be told what to be as a child. (Acts 20:32) A woman who has been in bondage all of her life can help others through Scripture. So now, brethren, I commend you to God and to the word of His grace, which is able to build you up and give you an inheritance among all those who are sanctified.

In the tools that I have shared and learned about looking within yourself, identifying your own trauma, and processing how to let go of the anger, guilt and shame that you have experienced. The tools you use can help you release the bondage that you may feel in staying stuck in grief and not moving forward. (Ephesians 6:10-13) Finally, be strong in the Lord and in his mighty power. Put on the full armor of God for your healing, so that you can take your stand against the devil's schemes. For our struggle is not against the authorities, against the powers of this dark world and against the spiritual forces of evil in the heavenly realms. Therefore put on the full armor of God, so that when the day of evil comes, you may be able to stand your ground and after you have done everything, to stand.

Culture teaches us it is more blessed to receive than to give, but God teaches us it is more fulfilling to give. If we accept the challenges that we have endured, learn from them, and release the anger they have caused within us, it can help us choose a healthier lifestyle and also reach out to others to share how we were able to move past the hurt and pain. Hurt people, hurt people, but if we choose to learn from our mistakes and make different choices, we can help others, not hurt them.

Don't be mad at somebody that said goodbye to you. It is part of life. People come in and out of our lives, and it is all about different seasons. As we grow, other people either grow with us, or sometimes they have their own paths (Acts 21:1–6). Faith is a journey of new friends and old friends.

The Holy Spirit is working to prophesy. I hear God's voice in meditation, prayer and when I stop my activities.

The Lord already knows what people are going through. God is all knowing, he has an understanding of what we go through in this "earth school" having lived as a human being experiencing our struggles of temptation, pain, hurt, and rejection. We need to accept that we are adequate as individuals and have a purpose here living on this earth. Life is not easy, and God understands our challenges that we endure on a daily basis.

When we are working as prophets for Christ, we need to request the Holy Spirit to guide us in what to say to people we are speaking to and witnessing. As an example, I have to stop myself on a continual basis when I get triggered to respond too quickly, and say the wrong words that might damage a relationship, give someone the wrong impression, and not speak kindly during a difficult conversation.

I have learned this lesson predominantly in the work environment when I am in a discussion on a confrontational phone call or expressing myself in emails.

It is not easy to take the emotion out of our conversations and written communications, but we must learn how to do so in order to present ourselves as prophets.

We need to be able to read the signs of the times; this is written in the Bible. (Matthew 1:37, 46-49) Those who treasure up the scriptures, which contain the signs of the times, will not be decided; they will be ready for the Savior's Second Coming.

In our difficult times, we need to accept these times as a gift of suffering, like what Jesus experienced here on earth. We are not to live for ourselves, but for the One who died for us. For me, I choose to accept what opportunities are presented to me whether they are an illness, a difficult work project, and the loss of many loved ones. It is hard for us to accept our challenges in life, but if we keep them in perspective, in knowing there is "purpose in the pain", it can help to endure the hurt we feel.

Women must refuse to compete with one another. It is our job to stand shoulder to shoulder. We need to give words of affirmation to each other and help each other through difficult times and not judge or try to be better than each other. We are all created as equals. I am part of a Women's Networking Group, *Women in Electronics*. We promote diversity, mentoring, and have various speakers throughout the year and at our conference to help support women in our industry.

Our goal should be to love Jesus with our WHOLE selves. In the practice of Holy Yoga, I take the time to start with the intention that my body needs to relax, forget about the stress outside the room, and focus only on the blessing of my organs, breath, limbs and muscles.

If we focus on the gift of our human body and our ability to be able to breathe in the air that God has created for us, and stay positive and thankful for our bodies, it helps to set a good intention for the goal of living for Christ, not ourselves.

We need to avoid disruptive cycles in the patterns of our life choices. For me, I continued to choose the wrong partners, experience stress at work, and not accept the challenge of dealing with difficult people as an opportunity to learn how to take the emotion out of communication with confrontational people in my life.

I continued in the disruptive cycle of seeking acceptance, love and this ideal "life living with a white picket fence". I was so concerned with looking good, feeling good, and making a lot of money.

Our testimony should be what is God's hand in the pain. As an example, when I lost my husband suddenly, this was one of the most difficult experiences I endured. I can now look back and realize that the positive aspect of this pain that I experienced when I lost Biff, was that I did have the opportunity to fall in love, and have an authentic relationship with a man that truly loved me. Biff accepted me, and cherished me. I believe God's hand in experiencing this pain after the loss of Biff was showing me that this true love can exist.

I had continued to search for the wrong partners in my life, ignoring the signs that the relationships were self centered and not partners that God had chosen for me. I believe God brought Biff and I together, and although short in duration, our relationship fulfilled my desire to experience true love.

Paul's purpose was to testify to the gospel of God's grace.

One of my favorite scriptures is (Matthew 6:11) Included in the Lord's prayer is the petition, "Give us this day and our daily bread".

We need to acknowledge that our "daily bread" comes from God. We all have needs each day and if we recognize that these needs are provided by the Heavenly Father, it helps us to keep in perspective that God is the provider. We need to focus on one day at a time and that each need that we have on a daily basis is provided by God.

We must think differently to live differently. If we memorize Scripture to keep our minds renewed, victory can be achieved one day at a time.

Our Lord states, we shall know the truth, and the truth shall set us free. We are not to self-destruct. We need to stay focused on the fact that we need to live with the mindset that we are here to be a positive inspiration to others and share the truth of the knowledge of the gift of the Holy Spirit that can give us the utmost peace should we choose to accept his gift of eternity.

God will soon crush Satan under our feet.

We need to forgive people that did not live up to our expectations.

If we focus with intensity during our alone time with Jesus, we will discover what the single most important thing is that we were set out to do in this life.

(Ephesians 2:10) The Lord will rescue us from evil deeds. Good deeds express thankfulness to God.

(Titus 2:14) This change of heart through faith and the desire to do good deeds in thankfulness to God is accomplished only by God himself the Holy Spirit. God wants us to be eager to do good deeds for him

We live yards away on planet Earth. It is a cold, dark, evil world we live in with accidents, tragedies, cancers, death, etc.

(Hebrews 4:12) For the word of God is alive and active. Sharper than the double-edged sword, it penetrates even to divide soul and spirit, joints and marrow; it judges the thoughts and attitudes of the heart. We must stand up, draw the sword of the Spirit, shield of faith, breastplate of righteousness and the full armor of God. We are to be more than overcomers in Christ Jesus. We will be delivered safely at home. This is the absolute gospel truth.

Gratitude helps us live in the present and decrease our anxiety and increase our spirituality.

This can help us to decrease our desire for materialism. We need to open up our eyes to be thankful for difficult people, as they build character in us.

I have plaques and motivational pictures all throughout my yard and inside my house to help me to stay focused on having gratitude for life and the blessings that we all have here on earth. One example of a plaque I have on my fence in my yard states, "Smile often, give thanks and love others." I spend a lot of time outside and do my writing and bible study outside. This gives me the opportunity to listen to the birds, watch the wildlife, watch the sunset and sunrise to enjoy the beautiful desert that I reside in.

We need to be thankful that we have family members, even if they don't act like we want them to. Gratitude is simply looking for the good. It is a choice. God saw that it was good, and it was good. (Genesis 1:31) God saw everything that He had made, and behold, it was very good and He validated it completely. It is a language of heaven when God speaks. Our innermost attitude changes when we look to the good and find God.

Jesus came to this earth to teach acceptance and kindness and love. I want people to feel this way when they are spending time with me. I have stayed in the corporate world to provide for my family and earned good income that has provided me the ability to travel, wear nice clothes, buy jewelry, expensive homes and cars; but in the end, it has not filled my spirit with the love that Christ wants me to show to others. I will continue to work on finding the balance of my work assignment and identifying my life's purpose.

I have experienced loss, being falsely accused, and the trauma of being judged throughout my career, but working in the corporate environment has taught me how to move past the feeling of being unaccepted and unappreciated.

I have used the tools that I have learned in my personal life to learn not to take people too personally, as they may also have experienced their own trauma in life. Daily practice of Holy Yoga, meditation, and reading scripture has helped me during my time at work to keep the challenges in perspective. I am able to accept dealing with difficult people, encountering chauvinistic people, and being ridiculed for my strong personality

Monetary compensation has been of great importance to me in my "survival mode" that I have been in for over fifty years. I watched my parents self-destruct, lose their health, money, and security.

I witnessed my father losing all he had and choosing to continue to self-destruct with alcohol and drugs and cigarettes. It would sadden me as a little girl when I could hear my father coughing in the next room, knowing that we will always only have two lungs and that we need to protect the body that God has created for us here to serve. I watched my father endure six years of cancer, several surgeries, and being admitted into a VA hospital for several months.

In 1978, my father went into remission from his cancer. We immediately moved away from the rat race of LA city life into the middle of the desert. I lived on dirt roads with no friends for me to play with when I was entering fourth grade as an only child.

It was a lonely time, but I learned to walk miles throughout the desert, introduce myself to all the neighbors, play with lizards, watch coyotes in packs running through the desert, roadrunners scurry across the dirt roads in front of me in over 100-degree heat over two months of the summer.

I have spent my whole life seeking security by striving to make more money, obtain important titles, buy expensive homes and cars, and this false sense of security has only brought more anxiety. In all of my teaching, prayers, meditations, and Bible studies, these activities have shown me to trust God for my life lessons that I will continue to learn throughout the remainder of my years here on earth.

I did not feel safe in my own body as a young child, so I continued to search for material things to try to fulfill the false sense of security of not feeling safe or protected. Life is a process, and we need to learn from our mistakes and how to do the work of learning how to feel safe in our bodies. I had mentioned the life work that I have done with Dana, my spiritual counselor, of envisioning myself in my body of being safe, not abused or traumatized.

I use burning sessions to help release the anxiety that I have during the day. It is so important to release the anxiety out of our body and minds. I write down the circumstances of challenges that I am currently experiencing, for example, perhaps I had a challenging person I had encountered at work, had a disagreement, and am still experiencing frustration and anger.

I write down, "I burn and release to Jesus Christ", this particular challenge and release the paper into the fire and watch it burn. This is a symbolic exercise of releasing anxiety, anger and emotions that are not healthy for our mind, body and soul.

I have a plaque in my home that reads "Excellence is not a skill, it's an attitude." My daddy had a pin on his cowboy hat that said "ATTITUDE," and frequently lectured me on how much my attitude matters in life.

Although I have experienced many losses and trauma during the course of my life, I choose to place positive scriptures throughout my household, daily reading of scriptures, and listening to worship music to help heal my mind, body and soul.

I have struggled with keeping myself positive during trials and tribulations in life, but know that this is so important for all of us to keep it all in perspective. The only thing that has kept me reminding myself of the importance of this key strength is the love of Christ inside of me.

I was diagnosed with pneumonia in May of 2019 and this gave me the opportunity to really take a look inside while doing a Bible study entitled *"Embracing Purpose"* by Linda R. Slaton to come to the realization of WHO I AM. During this Bible study, I gained a better understanding of what I had encountered and studied how my choices of self-destruction were counterproductive to living the purpose for my life that God created me to be: a writer, yoga instructor, counselor, retreat coordinator, a high tech salesperson, and public speaker.

It has helped me to stay in attendance of daily bible studies to help me with learning about the purpose for my life. I learn what the bible says about dealing with trauma and difficult life experiences. (II Corin 5:7) For we walk by faith, not by sight. I believe that my faith in God has helped me to accept the challenges in my life.

The definition of acceptance can be understood in different ways to different people, depending on their point of reference, life experiences, and faith.

There is great purpose in my acceptance of what I have endured. I have the courage to step out in my faith, knowing that God will guide me through my next years of life to use these gifts and not stay wrapped up in my own identity crisis of who I really am. It's time for me to listen and learn more, then teach. We all need to learn how to love ourselves in order to properly love others the way God intended for us to love each other.

True love comes from Christ. This is agape love. The only way we are truly capable of showing and accepting this type of love is to have the Holy Spirit living inside of us.

Our Lord has a way of showing us reality when we are taken out of our day-to-day monotony of work and regular routines of life. I try to set time aside each day and reflect on what I am here for. Each day when

I experience a challenging work chore, dealing with difficult people, and not being able to solve a certain problem, I will stop my emails, walk away, pray, breathe, and surrender to God.

I believe I have been trying to prove to my dead parents that I can be this high-powered, independent, top sales corporate professional that could obtain a degree and achieve a six-figure income to show everyone that I am a survivor. This has not fulfilled me. In reality, what lights me up is the outdoors, spending time with friends that truly love me, my yoga practice, meditation, and worship. I think back to the experiences I had at summer camps growing up.

These times at camp bring back great memories of being in the Southern California mountains, meeting various christian counselors that helped to give me guidance and show me the love of Jesus Christ, singing camp songs, swimming and having fun. It warms my heart to think about these happy times of my life.

I know in my heart that I was put on this earth for a purpose: to share my faith and how I overcame trauma so others can too, and show that no matter what trials and tribulations we go through, we need to forgive, love, stay true to our faith, and understand that all things happen FOR us, not AGAINST us. I have discussed various tools throughout this book that I pray can help you for your own life challenges.

It is hard, living in this human shell, to remember that in all the pain, sadness, and loneliness, there is another side to grief. There is another side of this universe that we live in called heaven. I have been given the blessings of visions and dreams showing me and hearing the sounds of heaven and feeling the Holy Spirit. This, in and of itself, gives me comfort.

In life, we all have the free will to make our own choices. I have tried to control my own destiny and not trust in our Lord to guide me, but to force love and security. The first fifty years of my life have been challenging, but I would not be where I am now in this healing journey if I had not experienced what I have. I share my experiences in order to help others, such as orphans, widows, children of alcoholics and physical abuse, parents of children with issues, those suffering from celiac disease, and women with female issues.

We all must all make wise choices and believe in our own self-worth. For me, the stress of not believing my sons will get past their own challenges and become fine young men that are contributors to society has not given me peace within myself. I must trust that God has a plan for both of them for their own lives purposes.

When I am in the state of trying to fall asleep, I have been taught a mantra to state to myself, "I trust, I trust, I trust, I am light, I am light, I am light," and envision the true Christ center coming through my body to comfort me from above my head to below my feet, and truly believe it. I can be at peace knowing I have lived another day for God's plan for me in this lifetime.

My entire adolescent and adult life I have been told, "You are so strong." My strength does not come from me, it is the spirit within me. God has blessed me with this shell (my human body), that allows me to have the strength to endure all the pain and loss. In the Bible the Lord states, "When we are weak, he is strong in us. When we accept Jesus Christ into our hearts, this brings us the courage to endure the challenges given to us here in this Earth School.

There is a prayer of salvation that you can make to assist with accepting Jesus Christ into your heart. For example, you can pray, "Lord, I know I am a sinner. I know that I need you to help me accept the challenges in my life. I believe that you brought your son of God into this world to help us obtain forgiveness for our sins. Please help me to live the remainder of my life by putting you first in my life. I pray that I can learn your scripture that you have provided to me to help me understand your plan for my life."

I need to teach others how I was able to heal and have peace in my life. I am an advocate of motivational speaking, but only when it is not based on ego, but self-love and acceptance and the courage to accept the things they cannot change. I have sought out several teachers, women in leadership positions, spiritual teachers and yoga instructors to find this peace, but in all reality, this inner peace has always been there, I just needed to have the courage to stop and listen to the message being relayed to me my whole life.

I have struggled with self-confidence. I need to believe that I can be a good teacher. For many years I have been told that I was too strong, not patient enough, too focused, too pushy, and an irritation to people. I get frustrated when events and action items do not take place in my timeframe. I need to stay focused on meeting others where they are; it is not always about just my agenda. If I believe anything that is happening is wrong, I speak out about it, and generally am punished for it. I just need a little help with some gentle and quiet spirit guidance from God during my communication.

I need to have the courage to be who I am with confidence, clarity, and purpose, to share my message and abilities to endure my challenges with God's help and guidance and how others can too. I have never questioned my faith. I have struggled with truly trusting in God during life challenges and just letting things happen naturally instead of forcing them to happen. There are so many others that have experienced tragic loss, sickness, and heartbreaks. We all have a story, it's just how we choose to share it and what lessons we have learned in our lifetime. I pray that for the remainder of my life I can find the right words to express myself and be an inspiration to people.

## WISDOM

I have always enjoyed school and learning. I have discovered my gift of teaching. In my past position in corporate America, I was given the opportunity to train the sales team of the company globally utilizing what I had learned for over twenty-five years in the electronic industry. There can certainly be a direct correlation in anything we learn to life's lessons.

I want to take the years that I have learned from electronic engineers, supply chain managers, and C-level executives about building relationships, educating myself on product knowledge, how to serve customers, listen to what the actual value-added propositions would be for my customers to want to buy from me, and take this knowledge and transfer it to my passion for healing, comforting, sharing God's love, enjoying working within my body during my yoga practice, and using these gifts for my life's purpose: to give back.

The key in my next chapter of life will be to take this wisdom and the experiences, knowledge gained, pain endured, sorrow, and health issues, and envelop this learning into something positive for me to share with others so I can help them with their own challenges and be an inspiration to them and encourage them to keep going.

I enjoy movies on *Pure Flix*, the Christian movie channel, as I find they have a good message about Christ's true love for us. Many of the stories they show are true life experiences for various characters including abuse, death from drunk drivers, and loss of loved ones, showing forgiveness from those who were affected by tragedy.

I enjoy watching these stories, as I do believe God can work through them for us to learn and reflect on what our actual story is, and how we can write our own book to help others with the acceptance, courage, and wisdom for their own lives.

I would like to share that my Holy Yoga certification is one of my achievements that has helped me to learn to release control and find inner peace.

This type of yoga will give others the blessing to experience our Holy Spirit shining throughout our bodies, experiencing the true peace that only Christ can provide through us. Our bodies are vessels to show others how we can love ourselves and others by true acceptance.

The Lord works in mysterious ways. During my transition between jobs, I take the time to write, meditate, read, and try to discern what

God's plan is in all of the experiences I have had in the previous years and how I can take a step back and see what God's message is in each job position, experience, projects, and new people that I meet. My career has been my focus since I was seventeen years old, and God tries to show me that this is a vessel to work his plan for my life.

We all struggle with wanting to control things on our own without taking the time to listen to the Lord with his subtle hints and answers he gives us. God always knows best!

Life can be a constant transition, and I accept this fact.

I have had the opportunity to enjoy time off in between positions to enjoy rest, relaxation, self-reflection, healing, and seeking guidance for next steps. I will continue to do my self-work and discover how I can find true happiness and peace. An example of doing the self-work is finding a life coach or spiritual counselor that you can trust and help you to also identify what has caused you to make the wrong decisions for your life and not leading a healthy or productive lifestyle.

I had sought out various psychologists throughout my young adult life and they did not always help me discover why I was making the wrong choices. I believe it is important to find a counselor that can help you discover tools that can work for you from your specific challenges during your life.

The first fifty years of my life have been a consistent task of survival mode. I have had the opportunity to learn Scripture and incorporate yoga practice into my daily walk with the Lord, learning to truly meditate. I am now teaching two nights per week and hosting retreats, and it has given me a sense of accomplishment.

I have attended a few kundalini yoga retreats where we sit in a circle and share our struggles and work together in a shamanic journey with a spiritual animal to receive an encouraging message. In my opinion, this practice is not against Christianity, as some might believe this is opening ourselves up to the evil one. But my experience has actually given me a great opportunity to speak in my tongues, and I always see Jesus and his unconditional love, grace, peace, and comfort during these retreats. (Psalm 119:15) I will meditate on your precepts and fix my eyes on your ways.

During my dreams, I have seen my loved ones laughing and hugging me. I have seen the archangels Rafael and Michael and felt the presence of peace, healing, clarity, and comfort.

Griefshare is a program taught in church that helps others heal from being in a state of grief. I have functioned as a facilitator for this lesson. It was difficult to obtain attendees for the class, as many people grieving from the loss of a loved one hesitate to address their grief and attend a program that will give them the steps they need to move on from the pain and receive acceptance.

We are all different in our own way. I internalize my hurt and express myself in different ways. In therapy a counselor stated, "You are confusing, you seem to be so happy and jovial, but the choices that you make speak the truth about what you feel about yourself inside.

Serena, you choose people that are emotionally unavailable to you, because that is what you are familiar with." The male relationships I have chosen start with affection, gifts, communication, and seem to disintegrate over time. I isolate myself and stop opening up, for fear of them getting to know Serena and using that against me somehow. I can pretend to be this happy, positive, successful, and grounded person, but in reality, I am the same as many others that have experienced hurt and are still learning how to heal from it.

In 2020, I was awakened about 2 o'clock AM, and needed to use the bathroom. I crawled back into bed and lay down and there was a sharp object poking my back in bed. It had not been there before. I turned the light back on and looked under the mattress cover and there was a needle with white thread attached to it.

I had never sewed in this bed and am the only person that had slept in this bed. This was very peculiar to me, and I felt drawn to prayer and research to try to identify the meaning of this "message." I discovered that the meaning is, I am healing now in my life from my divorce and trying to understand how to heal and move past the hurt in the losses of my life and struggles with parenting. The white thread was described to me from God as purity and cleansing. I truly believe this object was placed in my bed for a message to me.

God works in mysterious ways through his spiritual guides and I have no doubt they are always with me. I feel blessed to have the experiences that I do and the openness to research the meaning and draw closer to Jesus in trying to understand the purpose of his messages to me.

We have the opportunity in this lifetime to be an example and stay positive and accept our challenges. I believe in the power of positive thinking, but I also know that for me, it needs to be a focus on God and his ability to give us the opportunity to change the way we are thinking and acting based upon our experiences. We are weak human flesh and it is not easy. I have read many books, enjoyed Wayne Dyer and Dr. Joe Dispenza teachings, and believe that there is a balance in managing the way we think, understanding how our brain works, identifying our actual thoughts, and how we can work in the human spirit to be a positive example to others.

I have connected with a few people in my life that I can honestly say have spoken to my spirit within and touched my heart. These people are a gift from God to me.

It is heartwarming to know that not only Jesus Christ is here, he has always blessed me with angels and spiritual guides to help me during my journey here on this planet. I am open to listening, envisioning heaven, and appreciating the beauty in nature.

I am a "water baby." The water brings my spirit to rest. I feel like a different person when I am walking on the beach. I have always enjoyed moving water. Listening to the sounds of water that is moving is healing. It gives us the appreciation of nature and how innocent life can be. When I am at home, I have a water fountain that I listen to to remind me of the sound of running water. Listening to the sound of water outside of my office window brings me peace and calms me when I am working on my emails. I also like using my phone and listening to apps with the sound of the ocean waves and rushing rivers.

It is so important to have the ability to disconnect from this earth and appreciate the spiritual realm of living and not focus solely on this planet, but our heaven here on earth that God has created. When I see the visions that have been given to me of life after death, it warms my heart to know that there is even more beauty, and a paradise that is unimaginable here with our brains and senses here in this human body.

I received the gift of spiritual tongues at the age of twelve. I was with a friend from elementary school and she began speaking in her tongues. We held hands and I repeated her tongues. Within a few hours, I felt like I was not on earth. It was a feeling of an out-of-body experience and I had my own individual spiritual language that I was speaking.

I know this to be factual and true, and I use my tongues periodically now and find my body swaying and not being in the state of mind that I would be in my regular existence on this earth. It is another "realm," so to speak. I use this language in deep prayer in speaking to Christ in asking him for support, love, comfort, and clarity. It is an ongoing process.

I thank God for the ability to have this gift and pray that I will continue to learn from it, and heal by using this special language that God has blessed me with in this human experience. (1 Corin:14:27-28) If any man speaks in an unknown tongue, let it be by two, or at the most by three, and that by curse; and let one interpret. But if there be no interpreter, let him keep silence in the church; and let him speak to himself, and to God. It is okay if you do not receive this gift of tongues, it is a spiritual gift that only certain people are given. We all have the capability of praying to God.

The gift of spiritual tongues is a personal language that is given to some people to communicate with God. We can all pray to God at any time to communicate with Him at any time. God is open to communication with us at all times.

Singing has always given me great joy. (Psalm 9:1-2) I'm thanking you, God, from a full heart, I'm writing the book on your wonders. I'm whistling, laughing, and jumping for joy; I'm singing your song, High God. I am blessed to be attending a church that has given me the comfort and spiritual experience during praise worship that helps me stop thinking about my worries of the world. When I am sad or frustrated from the week, I attend my church and sing worship songs.

Listening to christian music lifts me up. I feel a sensation in my body that is joyful and I release the frustrations from my week to God and sing to him in thanksgiving that he forgives, brings comfort, and gives me the ability to release to Him and feel His presence while listening to the words in worship music.

When singing, I truly focus completely on Christ and what he has done for me. From the time I was in elementary school, I listened to Carly Simon, Olivia Newton John, and Helen Reddy. I have enjoyed karaoke and singing for my friends in a social atmosphere, but what brings me the most joy is singing out to Jesus in church and when walking on the beach by myself. Summer camp in the mountains of Southern California has been a good memory for me in learning different worship songs and praise music.

I have shared many different lessons that I have learned and tools that I now use to help me with my anxiety, grief and health issues. We all need to find a way to identify what can bring us peace within the chaos of living here in earth school. It is important for all of us to look within, and identify what really lights up our heart, gives us strength and endurance, and find ways to still have a positive attitude and acceptance of what has happened to us. For me, my belief in Jesus Christ and studying biblical scriptures has given me clarity and a good understanding of how to move forward and stop looking for the "white picket fence" as my perfect life that I had created for so many years that did not bring me the fulfillment and joy that I had continued to look for in men, relationships and my work environment.

# ELEVEN

# Going Home

In December of 2016, when I told my husband that I wanted to take the transfer back to California and my children's dad and grandma said they would move back as well. I was going home! This decision was the turning point of my life.

I have been blessed with a career that has given me the opportunity to travel to beautiful places and meet new people. I am now in a good place. I'm living at home in Southern California where the beaches reside, the mountain air is a quick drive away and the beautiful clean desert air is available to me.

California will always be my home. I shared my life with my parents there, birthed both of my children, bought my first home, and found Jesus Christ in the beautiful desert that I grew up in. I especially enjoy the wildlife in the desert and mountains. I can go to the beach and feel my father's presence, enjoy my church home, and visit my long-term friends that I have known for over 40 years that have been there to support me, love me, and accept me for who I am.

I have moved in a different spiritual direction since the return home to California.

The Lord speaks to me in dreams and through spiritual healers. I received a phone call from a buyer that I had worked with before Biff died.

She stated that she had a hunch things were not right for me and I was not happy. A few months later, she witnessed a magnet that I had given her on the refrigerator fall right off in front of her on its own. She then said she knew she had to call me and tell me she knew something was wrong. It was a sign.

I had another buyer call to tell me she had a message from my mom. "You are not listening! Serena, don't sacrifice like I did; you need to make changes in your life."

Where I reside today, Biff is there. He knows I talk to him.

I received validation from the Lord at the time of my decision to move back to California that there was a door being closed and I would be opening a new one. I need to be open to change and allow myself to downsize. Now was the time to take care of myself.

After I have dreams, I pray and study the meaning as best as I can understand the message that I am being given. The symbology of flying and large tools can give me a message of wanting freedom, and providing me tools to help me through difficult times. In my dreams, I am shown that I need to honor my life as a gift and accept the tools that I am shown and use them to help me persevere and grow from my challenges. I need to accept all the heartaches, and have faith. I would not be standing and alive in this world without my faith. I praise God for the gift of the dreams I have been presented with, giving me validation of the right decisions I have made for my life in the last five years, home in California.

# TWELVE

# The Turning Point

On June 3, 2017, when I left the Austin, Texas, area to relocate to California with my older son, Jaden, it was one of the best decisions of my life. My younger son did not move with me, as he chose to stay with his father in Texas. This was a tough decision for me, but I thought he would be back living near me shortly thereafter. I knew there would be a plan for him.

Prior to me leaving in June, I went to see my spiritual counselor Jayne and she gave me the clarity that I was making the right choice for my transition. In our session together, my mother came through again to state, "You are not listening, Serena. LET IT GO."

I can give my children my love and do the best I can, but in the end, these are God's children too. They will have their own path. It was so hard for me to let this go. I received all kinds of free advice from people asking how I could leave my son behind. This was not by choice, and it hurt for both of us.

At the completion of my session with Jayne, I had clarity to see the reality of my confusion, feelings of defeat, and judgment of myself as a mother.

The various sessions I have had with both Jayne and Dana have given me comfort in knowing there is another life beyond this existence here on earth. There is a spiritual realm.

God always has a plan for the trajectory of our lives. If we choose to stop and listen to His guidance, life can have a much better outcome. I find that when I get stressed I use curse words, I am impatient, and I tend to lash out and get sick. This is not a productive lifestyle. I struggle with burying myself in work to avoid not stopping to just BE. The practice of Christian yoga helps me. Meditation and prayer help me as well. I enjoy talking with like-minded people who trust God, are not led by fear, and are learning how to be healthy with themselves, not relying on a relationship or other crutch to fulfill their dreams.

# THIRTEEN

# On To Healing

Today is here and tomorrow will come and go. With vision, belief, and discipline today success, joy, and happiness will come your way. The future you live in is the future built today.

I consider myself a Christian woman with expanded spirituality. Here are some components for good relationships:

1. Safety
2. Trust
3. Vulnerability
4. Honesty
5. Respect
6. Regard (holding others as higher)

It is with constant review of these qualifications for good relationships that I thank God for the wonderful friends I have had all my life to help me through tough times. I had one cousin and four very special friends fly to Austin to come be with me when I lost the love of my life.

I have mutual friends that have experienced dealing with difficult special needs children that can talk to me without judgment or criticism, and have understanding of my heartache during the tough decision to send my child away to a Christian boarding school.

We all are here on the planet for a short time and I believe there is a purpose for every existing human being. It does not surprise me that all of the massacres, 9-11, earthquakes, and hurricanes are happening. It is written! I spend a large portion of my free time reading the Bible and trying to understand life here on this planet and what the meaning of the afterlife is. The book of Revelation is one of my favorite books in the Bible because it talks about what will happen when we get to leave this world to be with Christ in paradise if we chose to be a part of God's family.

I choose to live by the biblical Scripture and study it each day to learn more about what God's plan is for this world and how to live like Jesus Christ as best as I can. We all sin and fall short of the glory of God. It is hard to stay consistent in our trust. Jesus was unselfish, loving, not judgmental, and he came into this world, as God in person, to help people, even while we were all yet sinners.

The message the Lord keeps giving me is to listen. He speaks to me during my sleep state predominantly. It can be difficult sometimes for us to understand the actual messages God is giving to us. I have found that he can use one word as an example for me to try to decipher what the meaning of his message is for me. For instance, I was referred to two different job opportunities.

In prayer, I was continuously asking God to give me a sign as to which position to take, and the Lord continually kept giving me the specific name of the company that I eventually chose to work for. Initially, I was ignoring God's direction, and he gave me the answer by the other position being given to another candidate. Why don't I just listen?

I particularly enjoy the teachings of Rick Warren. I listened to a message from him in respect to how to know if God is actually speaking to us.

Rick Warren shares some of his teachings to test if the words you are receiving are from God:

1. Does it agree with the Bible? (Luke 21:33) states that truth does not change. Opinions and science are not constant. God's Word does not contradict itself.

2. Does this make me more like Christ? Jesus is the standard to evaluate every thought we have. He resembles purity, peace and love. Life is a test. God is more interested in character, not comfort here on earth.

3. Would it hurt anyone else? Wisdom from God is considerate, submissive, humble, and teachable.

4. Is it full of mercy? If we get an idea, is it forgiving? We need to be gracious towards others and not judgmental or harsh. We need to find the good in every person and situation. Wisdom from God is impartial and sincere.

5. Does my church family confirm it? For myself, I have particularly enjoyed being in the community with other women studying Scripture, but have typically been single and on my own raising my kids.

    I do not want to be judged, and have found God's love comforts me and gives me the guidance I need. God does not judge me, he supports me, and I have received Godly advice on how to love like Christ. Studying Scripture helps to obtain guidance on how to handle circumstances beyond my own understanding and to reach up to Christ. (Eph. 3:10) The wisdom of the righteous can save you.

6. Is it consistent with how God shaped me? Don't be somebody you are not. SHAPE:

    S = SPIRITUAL GIFTS
    H = HEART
    A = ABILITIES
    P = PERSONALITY
    E = EXPERIENCES

This determines what function we are. We are God's workmanship. He created us all to do good works and our shape determines our purpose.

7. 7. Does it concern my responsibility? It is not our job to be God; we do not need to worry about what others think (Rom. 1:4). God will use us to confirm what he has already stated to others, and sometimes when you hear something and someone else randomly states those same words, it is a confirmation that it came from God. We need to be patient and pray. We are unconscious to some of God's words at times.

8. 8. Is it convicting rather than condemning? Conviction comes from God. Condemnation, accusations, and hatred come from Satan (Rev. 3:19). We need to be earnest to repent and change our attitudes (Rev. 12:10). Satan is the accuser of believers.

9. 9. Do I feel God's peace about it? Confusion and pressure do not come from God. I am an over-thinker and I analyze so much when I pray and spend time with God. God teaches us to not get caught up in ourselves (1 Cor. 14:33). Satan wants to drive us compulsively and discourage us.

Ninety percent of what God wants to say to us is encouragement. His peace will be with us when we do and act on what we hear from him (Prov. 22:7). Listen to wise advice. He who belongs to God hears what he says to us. It is a blessing to be God's children.

I visited Israel in 1999 with my church and the holiday of Easter has always meant so much more to me in standing near the hill where Christ was crucified and walking Golgotha envisioning the pain and agony that Christ experienced on this planet just to save our souls. When I experience sadness, loss, tragedy, sickness, difficult children, or divorce, it is nothing in comparison to what Christ endured on this planet for our salvation.

Upon standing in Capernaum in the cathedral, I could feel the Spirit moving in that place where Christ cast out the demons of the little boy.

We are all subjected to demons. (Matthew 12:22-50). Jesus casts out a demon from a blind and mute man, then teaches about blasphemy, the fruits of the heart, peoples' desire for signs, and relationships.

I do not consider myself religious, as the traditional denominational churches do not appeal to me. I do not believe that God had intended for the Church to be one of rituals to comply with what people think is the right thing to do.

I attend a church to serve, learn the Bible Scriptures and how I can incorporate the teachings into my daily living, and fellowship with other like-minded people who also believe Jesus is the Son of God who died for our sins for us to receive forgiveness and salvation and eternal life (Matt. 25:41,46). (In fact, if you say that aloud and believe it in your heart, you too can be saved.)

The Church, in my opinion, should not be about judgment. My relationship with Jesus is about learning how to experience agape love. True, unconditional love. The Church is God-loving people. Jesus Christ came to this earth to atone for our sins and earn our forgiveness. We have the opportunity to be disciples of him. There are eighty-six thousand seconds in one day. We need to use this time for good.

I have my daily devotion every morning and write down daily scriptures and I attend weekly bible studies and have studied various women's bible teachings to include, *He speaks to Me, Preparing to Hear from God* by Priscilla Shirer. Beth Moore and Kelly Minter have various bible studies that you will find as well. These studies have helped me to stay committed to a daily devotional and staying in the scriptures and learning how to live my life for God, not myself.

Even with all the heartache and pain I have had my entire life, I do not question God's intention.

I titled my first book, *God's Test Pilot.* I believe we all experience the tests that life has for us. Our life is a test that is given to us on a continual basis to provide love to those in need, endure hardship, and keep the faith, not turning our backs on God. Life has a purpose. It is not to be self-serving, but other-serving. It is easy to be selfish.

God created the earth, the heavens, and everything in it. (Genesis 1:1). We are in this human existence for a purpose. We happened for a reason. It is our job to search and discover why we were created and what our specific purpose is. We were created to be an extension of our heavenly Father here in "Earth School." (Psalm 139:13) For you created my inner being; you knit me together in my mother's womb. If we choose to not take life for granted, and really see the value of our specific human existence, it can give us joy in knowing that we matter and were created for a reason.

In this chaotic world, we will have trials and tribulations, but it is what we do with these experiences that matters the most. We are part of mankind and are created in the image of God. (Genesis 1:27) The creation of the world and human existence was not meant to be random (James 1:2). Consider it a sheer gift, friends, when tests and challenges come at you from all sides. You know that under pressure, your faith-life is forced into the open and shows its true colors, so don't try to get out of anything prematurely. Let it do its work so you become mature and well-developed, not deficient in any way.

God has a way of bringing people into our lives for a reason. I have such a diverse group of friends. I like to talk with people from different cultures, religious beliefs, and different careers.

I have been in the electronics industry since I was twenty-six years old, and have learned a lot about people. There are difficult people everywhere. I had a boss that would say to me, "Take the emotion out of it." I still struggle with this in dealing with difficult people, but will always remember this advice and have given it to others as well.

What has helped me tremendously is acceptance of our current circumstances. We can't question where we are, why we make the decisions we do, and who we are. We just need to be authentic within ourselves in knowing that God has a plan for every individual on this planet. Life is an opportunity.

Therapy has helped me throughout the years, but in reality, if I was not a spiritual person, I would not be in a good place. Here are some things I have learned in discussions with various friends and people that I have encountered throughout my life:

- It can be a challenge to just simply learn to be peaceful and happy. We need to learn how to be content. Happiness is a state of emotion.
- We need to learn how to find inner balance and the ways to self-correct when we are out of alignment; focus on inner peace, one-ness, and universal love. Getting out of the ego, etc.
- We are all spirits having a human experience. For example, I am infinite as a soul, but I am Serena Estes now, in this human body and human ego-consciousness.
- So while we are all alive in this lifetime, we are consistently both human and spirit, which means we have to learn to balance the two. You can't live your life from only a soul, higher-consciousness perspective. It's impossible. It would be a waste of the human life and human experience you have been given to do that. Instead, we have to find ways to marry the two together. For example, we need to find a practice that will help us experience mindfulness and living in the present moment. For me, this is the practice of Holy Yoga and meditation on scriptures. I use the bible app "Abide" each day to help me stop and listen to scriptures to help me with the anxiety that I experience each day.
- Each of us has a purpose in this lifetime to use our infinite, spiritual, deeper, all-one self as our home base of unconditional love, both inward and outward. We need to use this lifetime to be the best individual selves we can be. Our best selves are beings that make the most out of our time here, both for ourselves and for the people we come in contact with.

Mindfulness is so important in the practice of yoga and it is the communication to yourself that you are safe and secure and can experience joy.

Meditation can be difficult for many people, but when we can truly meditate and pray with Christ and clear our minds of nothing but God, it is a blessing. I believe that traditional yoga can teach us a way to learn to look within our own bodies and share love for ourselves and for our Christ.

In training for Holy Yoga, I shared earlier that we had the assignment to read *Eat this Book*. This book teaches the students how to incorporate the Holy Scripture into our practice and share with others our belief of Christ being the center of peace and love on earth.

If we slow ourselves down and exist in a meditative place before meetings, we will be received in a much more productive manner. I will need to inhale four times prior to any meetings with others. I will need to check in with myself and note how fast I am talking.

These are the lessons I have learned in my life here in Earth School:

- Restoration is possible after tragedy
- Loss is part of life, we need to accept it
- Go to God with an expectant heart for the next ten years
- Emotions are not bad. It is how you handle them that matters

Five things for Emotional IQ:

1. You know you have emotions
2. You know how to manage emotions
3. You have the capacity to motivate yourself
4. You recognize emotions in others (What is behind what they are doing?)
5. You can handle relationships

Emotional intelligence is four times more important than IQ. The definition of emotional intelligence according to the Oxford Languages,

111

*the world's leading dictionary publisher,* is the capacity to be aware of, control, and express one's emotions, and to handle interpersonal relationships judiciously and empathetically. Emotional competence separates strong leaders from mediocre ones. According to <u>Wikipedia</u>, the definition of emotional competence is the essential set of personal and social skills to recognize, interpret, and respond constructively to emotions in oneself and others. The term implies an ease around others and determines one's ability to effectively and successfully lead and express.

It is important when experiencing challenging circumstances, we must take the emotion out of it. We need to keep our emotions in check during communication and writing emails. It takes work to stop ourselves and slow down before responding. I have always struggled with this, as I have a tendency to want to just get the job done quickly and move on.

I have always had a deep voice. In many cases during my daily communication, I need to change the tone in my voice and this is a difficult task for me. I can have a sense of urgency in my voice and I am very passionate when I speak about a topic that I feel strongly about. I need to be mindful of my audience and pay attention to how I am conveying my messages to people.

I know I'm making a general statement, but when I slow myself down, it gives me the opportunity to step back and realize that no matter who I am communicating with, I need to be mindful of how I am representing myself. If I take the time to slow myself down before commenting or reacting in a negative way, then it can prevent damage control in the future.

If we are mindful and physically and slow ourselves down, the inner self will come. Anxiety drains away when we avoid negative thinking. In yoga practice, the focus is on the inner core being, breathing, and envisioning the inside of our bodies to be in balance and grounded.

One way that I can disconnect is during bath time. My therapist has encouraged me to use candles and bring them with me when I travel and take the time to bathe and relax.

When I am driving, I have muscle tension. I have struggled with back and neck pain since I was a teenager. I make it a point to get a massage once per month. I have a jacuzzi in my backyard and enjoy feeling my muscles relax, gazing at the stars, and disconnecting after a day of work or stressful meetings.

I believe it is so important for all of us to find what creates relaxation within our body for ourselves and be intentional in implementing these exercises in our daily schedule to alleviate keeping the stress within our bodies. I typically use visualization in my practice for my students, asking them to envision something that is pleasing to the eye, smells good, feels good and has a pleasant sound to them.

It is so important to be in a calm state of mind in every aspect of our lives, we need to be focused on being in the moment and have peace within ourselves instead of allowing our emotions to take over and causing ourselves unnecessary stress within our body. I realize this is difficult to stay in a calm state of mind at all times.

This has been something I have worked on my entire life, as I have a type A personality, and can react very quickly when I do not agree with someone or believe they are being arrogant or lazy. It takes constant focus on being cognizant of where we are focusing our energy. It needs to remain positive and not strained. How we modulate energy needs to be our focus.

One good example of a tool that can help to alleviate negative energy, is using a personal journal or having a place in your daily calendar to write about a difficult or positive experience we have had during our day. This exercise has helped me observe the way I am reacting to my life experience. At the end of the day, I pick a couple of moments from each day and write about them. I keep this journal at my bedside. I also have a separate booklet where I write down my dreams.

We need to be narrative and explain how we reacted in each experience. If we manage to zero in on the particular moment, sights, smells, temperature, it trains us to stop and absorb.

When we are eating our meals, it helps to not talk and rush through them. If we enjoy the flavors, experience the food, and appreciate the good taste and blessing of the food nourishing our bodies, it is a much more beneficial experience for us.

According to *Lee Holden*, a qigong instructor, he says, we should chew each bite 50 times according to qi wisdom. He says he chews 25 times.

I have not done a good job of appreciating my meals. I suffer from celiac disease and am limited as to the foods I can eat. I have been told I am allergic to gluten, dairy, eggs, soy, honey, lemons, sunflower seeds, and red meat. It is difficult to eat in restaurants, and it can be embarrassing for me to order a meal.

There are so many limitations on what I can eat and I do not want to represent myself as high maintenance, as it truly is a medical condition. My diet is not a fad, and there are so many others out there that do not order the food due to a medical condition, so when someone does it can be perceived as being a difficult patron. I pray that more people that work in the restaurant industry can educate themselves on food allergies and celiac disease to avoid their own frustration of serving those that suffer from eating. (Exodus 23:25) Worship the Lord your God, and his blessing will be on your food and water. I will take away sickness from you.

In the book *The Power of Your Attitude* by Stan Toler, he encourages us to make seven choices with the power to transform our lives:

1. Choose Hope
2. Choose Humility
3. Choose Gratitude
4. Choose Generosity
5. Choose Compassion
6. Choose Joy
7. Choose Perseverance

Toler states that positive thinking people choose an attitude of joy. They're eager to make the most of the day, whether it turns out as they plan or not.

According to Toler, happiness is a feeling you get when things are going your way. Joy is a deep-settled sense of well-being based on your positive outlook. Happiness fades away in minutes. Joy lasts a lifetime. Happiness depends on our circumstances. Joy depends on our attitude.

I read and listen to meditations daily, and enjoy learning how to motivate, stay positive, and set goals and objectives for myself. The first thing we need to do in the morning is get into a powerful mindset and a good mood. We need to set the gratitude in place before we even step out of bed. Each day is a gift and opportunity. I start my day by rehearsing the Lord's Prayer before I put my feet on the floor.

Daily exercise is key. I believe that if you add cardio and strengthening in your daily schedule this will help to alleviate stress and give yourself an opportunity to experience the appreciation of your body and heal within. An example of a daily schedule that I use is, I start my day with my morning bible study after praying the Lord's Prayer, go to the gym or take a 45 minute walk for cardio exercise, and then I stretch each limb using my yoga poses, using deep breathing exercises with calm music in the background.

It is imperative that we start each day with a grateful heart and give ourselves the time needed at the beginning of our day to set our mind in place to appreciate our body, mind and spirit.

Our bodies are vessels for us here in Earth School to give back, contribute, and appreciate the gifts of our eyesight, limbs, organs, heart, hearing, and the gift of breathing. Our minds need to be positive with expectations of a good day. If we say the mantra each day: "Today is going to be a great day, I'm alive, I'm awake, and I feel great!." This gives us an opportunity to start each day in a positive mindset, appreciate our bodies and look within ourselves each morning prior to starting our day in knowing that we can make the choice of our day to be productive, positive and meaningful.

We need to be appreciative of grace, mercy, wisdom, blessings, love, nature's beauty, wildlife, and sunshine. We will gain more from life every day if we choose joy.

In order to lead a productive lifestyle, many people believe that we need to be successful in our career choices, parenting and financial stability. There are many different ways to believe we are a success in life. "Success" is not convenient; we need to do what is required to be successful. If we focus on what is productive, profitable, and pursue our dreams, we will succeed in life. We must not blame anyone else, but take responsibility for ourselves and our choices. We need to do what we can to be an amazing person. We can get up early and get more out of life with the time that we are allotted each day. When we know what we want, the drive comes!

We need to honor our difficulties and struggles. If we want to have one of the best lives in the world, we need to work for it. Win in the morning! We don't waste time, and we don't compare ourselves to others.

For me, working in the sales environment my entire career, I have a tendency to be competitive and compare my achievements with others. We are all our own individual. We cannot lower our self-worth. We need to go straight for our goals and not be afraid of what others think.

In the motivational speaker world, many people can be discouraged and judged. We need to ignore these accusations and judgements, they are not healthy. If we focus on what impact we can have in the world, we'll have the key to obtaining our goals and objectives of being a good person and part of contributing to society.

The Lord speaks to me through visions and dreams, and I had a realization one day on my walk around Canyon Lake where I live. I was on my normal jaunt down the path alongside our pool, lakeside, and was given a strong sensation to go walk on one of the docks to lead me to the lighthouse that sits outside of our restaurant and lodge area.

The Lord spoke to me that there is a definite significance of a lighthouse. I do not typically notice lighthouses when I am at the beach or my local dock at Canyon Lake, but on this particular day, I felt like I was led to this area for a reason. I looked up the meaning of a lighthouse. According to *Webster's dictionary*, a lighthouse is a tower or other structure containing a beacon of light to warn or guide ships at sea.

A lighthouse can be a light that crosses the darkness and that comes into the dark world symbolizing hope. A light defeats darkness and can be considered the origin of a driving force that transforms unconscious contents and processes into conscious thoughts and feelings.

On January 2, 2021, I was told from the Lord to "reach the light". The message I received after my walk was the fact that what matters most is what we choose to light up for the world. It needs to come from inside of us. We need to search for the light within us and make it shine. We need to show our light to others, and share our story so it may help them. For me, no matter what storms or disruptive waters are around me, I will remain steadfast with my light shining from above.

I believe my job here in this earth school is to help explain how I can achieve the goal of continuing to have that light shine, no matter what danger or uncertainty lies ahead. The year of 2020 was uncertain, challenging, and many people suffered from anxiety, loss of jobs, freedom, and security, and losing loved ones to the COVID pandemic. This was another plague that we were to experience here to show us who is really in control. I believe this pandemic gave us the opportunity to find faith in God and surrender to him.

The lighthouse resembles the purpose of illuminating our way. We are never to choose or judge the path we take. We have our own path. This resembled my current circumstance of watching a loved one self-destruct and not enabling them to continue to take advantage of or blame others.

We all have this light that shines within us, but it is up to us to choose to turn it on. The lighthouse is steadfast, sturdy and reliable. Its purpose is to continually shine its light to safely guide the ships on their journey. But it is up to the commander of the ship to follow the lighthouse direction it is being led to.

As a mom, it is so hard to not want to just do the hard work for a lost child, but "tough love" is what we are taught by our leader for our lives, Jesus Christ. We are all given the choice of free will, the light that remains steadfast to give us guidance, but we have the option to turn the ship anywhere we want it to go.

We are given the "energy" of our own lighthouse to steer us in the right directions, but we must choose which way it will guide us. As a parent, we are the "light" for our children to show them how to walk, talk, behave and endure life, but each child can choose which direction he will follow the light. There are always alternative options to what are presented to us, it is up to us to choose.

The same day I was led to this lighthouse on my local lake, I was searching for a movie to watch and discovered one that was entitled *The Author, the Star, and the Keeper.* I had no idea it was a story of a man that was a lighthouse keeper. The message was about him bringing his son to the "light" to stop putting blame on the mother that left him and own his own choices for his journey. He chose fame, fortune, and an empty life when the light was being shown to him and the example of his father was right in front of him his whole life.

We all need to listen and find our inner guidance and the guiding light that is always surrounding us and leading our path. It is a matter of stopping to see the light. (Psalm 119:105) Thy word is a lamp unto my feet, and light unto my path. I have spent many years not paying attention to the light that was right in front of me.

I have sought out financial security, relationships that were not healthy for me, and made bad decisions to follow the wrong light to destruction. This was not the "white picket fence" that was made for me.

I believe God works and sends messages in mysterious ways. The same evening that I was shown the lighthouse, I got home and my golf cart lights were on. I had not turned them on. I heard the message, "Remember the light, Serena." I want God to illuminate my path on this journey here in earth school. I accept the challenge of following this light and stopping to listen to the message it is giving me.

There can be many different ways God can show you the symbolization of messages for you and give you the visibility of the challenges you have had and adversity that you have been blessed with to move past the darkness and seek the light wherever we go no matter what lies ahead.

We can have salvation and security and remain vigilant. We also need to stay alert and listen for any danger coming our way and pay attention to the storms of our life that will happen.

We need to remain in our faith in knowing that we have the guidance and support and salvation if we choose to follow the light in the right direction for our lives.

To me, the lighthouse represents Jesus Christ. He stands tall, gives light and direction, and we are part of this structure in him and have the responsibility to also be a part of giving the light to others and sharing how he gives us the right direction and who is leading us on the path.

I find that watching inspirational movies helps me to get the vision for myself that I want to have for my purpose. The movie *Wonder* spoke to my heart. This is a story of a little boy that is born with a birth defect and has a deformed face. Watching this movie helped me to realize that no matter what challenges or physical disabilities we may have, all of us have a purpose here living on this earth. This boy gave an example of a person that no matter what he had experienced, he chose to remain positive and accept his disability as part of his life and still remain in the mindset there was a specific purpose for his life. We all have our struggles, it is how we choose to address them that matters for our purpose in life.

At one point in my life, I did not drink any alcohol for six months of which I believe was the most positive decision I had made during this process of trying to decipher what my cure could be from these awful diseases that I have been diagnosed with for over twenty years. I believe God has always been nudging me to not drink any alcohol. I started drinking at age sixteen and thought it was fun and gave me the ability to "fit in" to the popular crowd and be the life of the party. Due to the fact both of my parents were alcoholics, I believe my desire for alcohol is hereditary.

I have considered myself a "social drinker". I now know that it hurt my body. Alcohol is a poison. We only have one liver, and it is a gift. Upon meeting with the holistic doctors, initially I would feel an improvement, but then it eventually just came back to the pain I was experiencing in my abdomen, diarrhea and bloating.

We need to integrate what works for our own body. We are all created with a different chemistry; what might work for you, may not be the program that works for someone else. I believe if we listen to our body, pray, and stay diligent with staying in the moment and seeking medical advice when needed, God will help us find the right answers.

One example of body symbology is when we experience bladder issues and infections, it can have the meaning of struggling with anger issues.

My goal every year is to slow myself down. In the past, I have been told I have an urgent look about myself. I am not present. I am high energy with forceful speech and physical presentation of myself. A yoga speaker with kindness, patience and peace is my goal of interpersonal communication with others. I believe people will respond to the yoga method of communication. An example of this method of communication is when I start my class, I set the intention of leaving any anxiety or negative emotions outside of the room. I state, "Let's leave everything outside of the room and breathe in positive energy, thankfulness and peace."

The Lord has shown me how to bring my spirituality and faith in God into my workplace. How I conduct myself in the business environment has a spiritual tone. I share about my faith in Jesus Christ and my license plate has "Bahleev" written on it.

I have been teased for advertising my faith on my car, but it does not bother me. I believe it can be a way to share our faith by sharing how we believe.

I am not one to continuously speak about Bible Scriptures or judge others by sharing about my faith making it sound like I am better than others, I just feel like God wants me to share how my peace has come after all the tragedies that I have experienced.

I believe we all experience different challenges in our lifetime, and it is up to us how we want to communicate to others about what has happened to us. I think it is very important to have the right attitude, stay positive, and acknowledge where our strength comes from after enduring our trials and tribulations.

I received a dream that showed me a title for my own business name, *One Heart*. In this dream, I was in a setting with my high school friends and we were preparing for an event. I was in the student council during middle school. Some of my fellow students spoke about their challenges they had endured in life. In this dream, I was given an opportunity to kick off a reunion and was asked to speak. I stated, "All of these challenges we have had are our own experiences here in earth school."

I shared with my friends that I have had great challenges and tragedies in my life and my parents were gone at an early stage in my life. I stated to them, "There is one thing that we all have in common in this life here on earth. We all have one human heart that beats to keep us alive in this human existence."

It does not matter what color, race, religion, or sexual orientation we are, we all still have this beating heart in common and share in the existence of being a human being living on planet earth. We all are to identify with this commonality of sharing a heart, and we need to be true to ourselves. I believe this dream gave me the clarity of my life purpose and mantra that I continue to share, "We all have one heart, a story and a purpose."

In my opinion, we all need to focus on what is in our heart and how we feel about what has happened to us.

We need to focus on our commonality and how we can connect with one another by sharing our stories, identifying any commonalities and sharing with others, and how we can use the knowledge that we have gained from the mistakes we have made and bad decisions we have made in our lifetime.

Every bad decision can make a good story. I believe every person should take the opportunity to share their own personal stories for the purpose of helping others identify their own story and what may be the purpose of life lessons that they were taught by their own experiences. There can be purpose in the pain that we experience.

After I awakened from my dream by giving myself the words One Heart, I felt this was a message from the Lord showing me this would be the name of my own company.

I was being shown by God how I could better understand all of my experiences in life and use them as an opportunity to share with other people to help them. The decisions I have made in life have contributed to my hurt, loss, grief, shame, anger, and mistrust. God's hand has been in all of it.

In my dream, I believe I was shown the big picture of how to share from my heart what I have learned from my life experiences. It is acceptable to make mistakes, learn from them, and release the hurt and fear to Jesus Christ. It is his to take. We can release all of it to his truth.

"For I know the plans I have for you, declares the Lord, plans to prosper you and not to harm you, plans to give you hope and a future" (Jer. 29:11).

God always provides, bringing opportunities and life experiences. It may take a lifetime to understand it, reflect on it, and learn from it, but that is okay. The important thing is to accept the opportunities given to us and learn from them.

I received insight from the book *The Untethered Soul* by Michael Singer. Mr. Singer teaches us how to find peace and happiness by addressing the voice in our head properly. We listen to our "voice" on a continual basis, but we are actually the observer of our own voice. Singer teaches us about awakening consciousness. We are spiritual beings inside a physical body with a mind.

Our thoughts that we say to ourselves are not us speaking. For example, when we say, "I'm not good enough," or, "I lost my job," we need to separate what we are not, and not get lost in the idea of what we are. We need to continue to stay out of the mind and pay attention to the emotions that come out of the heart.

Singer teaches us about the lucid self. We need to be aware of our mind, which is in constant motion, and understand the seed of our consciousness. This is something we are "watching," not something we are. We need to free ourselves from being the scared person inside of us. When we do this, it is considered spiritual growth. Our energy changes. We need to let go of who we think we are. We need to let it pass, or the energy will drag us down. We need to learn to relax and lean away from the noise in our minds and allow space. If we are connected to the Holy Spirit, this is where God flows through every moment of life, and this is a spiritual experience.

Fear is a thing. I had stayed in an unhealthy mindset for several years, not listening to the repercussions of staying in this mindset of fear.

Change is the very nature of life. If we harmonize with life, we don't take it over. We need to avoid trying to take control of our life. Fear does not allow us to do this. When we are watching ourselves, we hear the voice and take it into account; is it really giving us good advice?

Singer talks about the "inner thorn" inside of us that causes us pain.

Life is a spiritual journey and we are in constraint transformation. If we remove the thorn inside, we can enjoy life and experience the utmost peace. Events happen outside; we need to learn how to deal with the disturbance inside of us, and relax.

I pray for humility, patience, kindness, tolerance, gratefulness, forgiveness, peace, and love (Gal. 5:22–26). The Lord wants us to cooperate with the work he does in our hearts.

Friends are so important in life. The friendships that I have in my life have given me the tools to obtain the feeling of security, being unconditionally loved, and accepted for who I am and what I represent. I am very fortunate to have several long-term friends in my life that I consider my surrogate family members. I have a friend, Sunah, who has been in my life since second grade. We remained in contact after fourth grade when we moved to different states away from each other. We visited each other in the summer, wrote to each other, attended graduations and special events, and will always be close.

Sunah moved to America from Korea at seven years old and did not know any English. I was her first American friend. I will cherish my friend forever into eternity. She is gracious, compassionate, giving, genuine, and loving.

It is invigorating to really do some deep work within yourself and go back to facing the little three-year-old girl that lost her identity and felt unloved and unaccepted.

God is constantly at work in our lives. Sometimes we choose to not listen and have to take a step back to truly accept reality. It is a humbling experience.

Another exercise I had shared earlier in this book is the burning session release ceremony. I have been taught to write on paper to release guilt, shame, fear, and anger, and release it to the truth of Christ.

This exercise helps us with releasing these feelings by writing them down and releasing them. I physically burn the paper that I have written these statements on in regards to what I have felt guilty about, shameful of, and the people I have anger towards. This is a very healing exercise I highly recommend. (Of course, safety first; be aware of burn bans if you're doing this outside, and have a fire extinguisher at the ready at all times.)

I do daily meditation with two Bible apps, Abide and Calm. One message stated, "Obstacles do not block the path, they are the path."

Some inspirations I heard during some of these teachings include:

1. We are all God's children
2. Calm seas don't create sailors
3. Disappointment is God's appointment

The year 2018 was a year of reflection for me. I identified the word of the year to be *truth*. My goal was to identify my real truth.

I had been seeing Dana, my spiritual coach, in Orange County. Dana shared that her first impression of me was I was filled with my own ego. At first, I felt judged and ridiculed. I can now see that Dana was accurate in helping me to recognize I was working from the source of the unknown.

I needed to find my truth in order to understand the decisions that I had made to surround the source of information and block the trauma that I had as a child from the age of three years old.

The first assignment from Dana was to burn and release the light and truth that are not true and not serving my purpose of life, and getting me to a healthier place for a relationship, parenting, and identifying my true purpose of this lifetime, and perhaps my past experiences that my soul had encountered. The assignment entails actually writing down, "I release this guilt I have towards_____ _ " and physically burn each paper to really let it go and not try to control or hold onto the negative that is really not true for my life.

This exercise began in June of 2018 for me, and will be an ongoing process for the remainder of my lifetime.

Each day we experience challenges, lose patience, have anger towards people, feel ashamed, or try to control a situation, and we need to physically write it down, burn it, and release it to the truth.

The burning exercise is an opportunity to learn from the emotions and not let them envelop our minds and hearts but to truly give it back to the actual truth of what it is that causes these negative emotions. These emotional feelings do not serve us as productive parts of our society and hold our souls back from trusting.

I have always identified as a Christian and true believer that Jesus Christ is the son of God who came here to save us from our sins and allow us the opportunity to choose truth.

If you are encouraged by this message that you can be healed from your past, you are always loved, and there is an eternal life that is available to you after you leave this earth, you can say the prayer to God, asking for forgiveness for your sins, and accepting Jesus Christ was sent by God as the savior for forgiveness of your sins, and believing there is salvation for you.

I highly recommend the book or watching the movie, *The Case for Christ*. This book was written in 1980 by Lee Strobel and is a true story about his life as an investigative reporter that earned a promotion as a legal editor at the Chicago Tribune.

Things at home aren't going nearly as well. His wife Leslie's newfound faith in Christ compels Lee to utilize his journalistic and legal training to try and disprove the claims of Christianiy, pitting his resolute atheism against her growing faith. Strobel interviews 13 biblical scholars who assure him that the accounts written about Jesus's life and ministry, the ones accepted by church officials as canonical, are absolutely true. He becomes a christian and believer in Jesus Christ.

What I believe we continue to do is base our lives on the self-serving purpose of not looking at the actual soul as what we need to work on in our existence. Many people go through their lives without believing here is a soul in existence inside of us here as human beings and an afterlife. Many folks want "proof" that a soul exists.

For me, the truth of the story of Jesus Christ, the miracles he performed, and the fact that he rose from the dead gives me an absolute understanding that life here has a purpose and that Jesus Christ is in fact the son of God that was brought here on earth to save us from our sinful lives to accept forgiveness and live a life in eternity after our work is done here on earth.

The soul never dies; it remains alive and continues to try to teach us truth and how we exist in a happy "shell," understanding the purpose and reality of what our true identity of ourselves really is. It is not the physical being, it is our souls that God wants us to live for and learn from. We are given an opportunity in each lifetime to experience hurt, love, loss, happiness, appreciation, thankfulness, and truth, and these are all things that are a gift as part of our journey of our lifetime on this planet living as human beings.

Each generation has a lineage that we can look back and learn from to better identify why we do the things we do, how we think, what our ancestors lived for and how they made decisions. We may ask ourselves, "Was there an addiction? Abuse? Love? Good or bad parenting? Did our ancestors experience the truth?

Was there any native heritage or spirituality with our ancestors?" I am now at a place where I want to discover what my lineage is from both sides to try to better understand what my parents' and grandparents' point of reference was for their own lives, and was the pattern ever broken if there was abuse or addiction. I have inquired with relatives if my past ancestors were children that were shown love, and if they experienced loss, tragedy, or sudden death.

If we spend time learning what our point of reference is and what our ancestors' frame of mind and lessons were, it can certainly help us identify why we make the decisions we do. I have spent a great deal of my life not taking into account that I have blocked the tragedy and abuse that I encountered as a young child. I choose to now love myself, and actually have the ability to look in the mirror and say, "I LOVE YOU," and mean it.

I did not feel safe in my own body and have conducted myself as that little, three-year-old girl that was taken advantage of, physically and emotionally abused, and neglected. I had accepted this as a normal way of living my life. I have chosen relationships in my life that have served that same reality that it is not okay to be loved or love myself properly. I convinced myself I was not worthy of real, true love, and continued to seek love from the wrong people and partners.

In March 2019, when this world experienced the COVID pandemic, I believe this event taught us to take a step back and realize what is really of true importance for our purpose of existence here on earth. This experience was tragic for so many people in the world. I am a social person, and it was so difficult to not have the ability to hug others, speak to them in person, and simply go outside of my home without risk of dying or infecting others. I had just relocated to a small, one-bedroom apartment twelve hundred square feet less than my last townhome. This was quite the adjustment for me to dwell in such a small home. My older son also lived with me at this time.

I believe God gives us signs from heaven to show us he is the ultimate in control, not us.

It was apparent to me that the third week in quarantine we had earthquakes in California, tornadoes in Texas, and random rainbows throughout the country. I believe the Lord was showing us the power and glory he has throughout the universe. This pandemic gave us an opportunity to stop and reflect on what really matters in the grand scheme of life.

During this time of the pandemic, upon driving through the town and on the roads to the beach I witnessed all beaches, parks, trails, and public areas displaying closed signs, and even the grocery stores having armed guards to ensure that none of the local citizens were out spreading germs and staying respectful of not possibly being infectious and spreading this terrible disease. This really gave me perspective in knowing how grateful we should all be to have a home, a safe place to live, food to eat, clothes to wear, and let's also not forget the clean air to breathe with the void of cars on the road.

It was during this time that I looked up at the vibrant, blue sky and could see the visibility without all the smog and fast-paced, stressed people driving to their next destination.

I feel blessed to have experienced watching our lives slow down, being quiet, and witnessing those helping others obtain food, toilet paper, and the basic essential needs. We were forced to stay focused on the bare necessities that we really need. In all the quietness, it showed me what the true purpose of life should be, and the basics of survival. Love, kindness, gentleness, peace, and serenity were truly understood. People had no choice but to stop and realize all the material things and possessions that we really do not need had no meaning at all when it came to basic survival.

I was able to take more time throughout my freedom from travel, stress, and constantly being in work mode. I was able to pray, exercise, take walks in my immediate neighborhood, smell the flowers, listen to the birds, feed the ducks at my small pond, and read my Bible to learn more about what Jesus taught us. (1 Corin 13:13) And now these three remain: faith, hope and love. But the greatest of these is love.

My younger son returned home from boarding school on Easter of 2020, during the quarantine. He was able to live in our two homes between myself and his dad and spend time with his brother.

After fifteen months in boarding school, he came home to a structured environment and discipline in my home which was honestly a true blessing to see, knowing he found peace within himself and discovered the true purpose of his own life.

He stated that he did not need much, and just wanted to work, finish high school, join the AirForce, and buy a car. I had hoped and prayed that upon his return after this boarding school I would be able to spend time with him and have a positive experience. I pray someday my son will look back and see that as hard as it was for his mom to send her baby away to try to find healing and focus, it was from love and surrender to let the Holy Spirit find my boy away from his distractions and struggles.

It can be hard to let go and surrender a decision to God, knowing that from the exterior people all have their opinions and try to make you feel guilty because they do not see the value in your decision.

We have decisions to make throughout our lives and a plan from God that he has set for us to live a prosperous and effective life, but we all make our own decisions with our free will of choice. I took this time at the age of fifty-two years old to take a step back and not make quick decisions that could damage my long-term trajectory of a life here on earth. God has planned for me to be a vessel for him, to share my story and lessons that I have learned from making the wrong decisions.

Every decision is a choice. Life here on earth gives us the opportunity to stop and listen or make quick, damaging decisions that affect us in our lifetime and cause hurt and pain. It is so important to take the time to be alone, reflect, pray, and meditate on what is good, learn how to love unconditionally, appreciate the blessings of life and the goodness, and hear the sounds of nature, the voice of God, and just breathe in the blessings that life can bring to us.

As Wayne Dyer teaches, we spend so much time looking at the exterior, and ignore the interior, when all that really matters long-term is not things, possessions, but health, love, kindness for others, and making a difference by helping others and teaching them about the love that you can achieve inside of yourself. If we do not achieve that love within ourselves, we self-destruct.

# FOURTEEN

# My Message:
# Taking It Public

In 2019, I turned fifty-one years old. It was a time to reflect on my life and put it into action. I needed to craft my message and make it public by sharing my story and encouraging others to find peace and purpose in pain. We all have a story, and I identify us to be God's test pilots. What I mean by God's test pilot, is that we all have our own challenges, hurts, pain, frustrations and are given the opportunity to seek God in these trials and tribulations we experience during this lifetime. I encourage you to read my first book, *God's Test Pilot*. I hope that my two books I have written will bring encouragement to others that have also suffered with struggles in life here in earth school.

If we look to God for our strength and accept the fact that it is part of life to endure our challenges, it can give us a better peace and understanding that these challenges can be a gift from God to experience loss and pain. Because Christ willingly bore that pain, believers have the benefit of forgiveness and eternal salvation, which is God's purpose behind Christ's pain. Christ's testimony that suffering can come to us so that God might ultimately be glorified. (John 9:1-3 and 11:1-4)

As a believer in Christ, I accept the challenges that I have experienced in this lifetime, and know that there is purpose in the pain I have endured.

God always has a plan and I use this term "test pilot", as we all have this opportunity to seek God and work for Him.

We need to use the opportunities that are given to us to remain strong and share about how we were able to move past the hurt by trusting in God and releasing the frustration we can feel while going through difficult times.

The choice is ours to do something to help others in our message, or to exist and not give back. We have the opportunity every day to go out in the world and share and show love, joy, peace, happiness, and encouragement to others.

I have written two books to share the details of my stories, experiences in my relationships, losses, sickness, and struggles in corporate America. But truly, God does give us the serenity to accept the things we cannot change, the courage to change what we can, and the wisdom to know the difference. I know I cannot change my past, but I can have the courage to share my story with others and show them how I have remained strong, faithful, found peace in the pain, and happiness in being alive another day to experience what God will give me as my next opportunity to help others here in Earth School.

I was blessed with a dream on July 20, 2019 that gave me clarity in addressing my fear and for next steps in getting my message out to the masses. It gave me direction for sharing my story publicly and using the lessons I have learned and the work I have done using various tools to help others.

At the time of my dream, I was presented with the opportunity to create a speaker reel and package to start my business of developing health and wellness workshops and speaking engagements to share my story. My fear of the lack of money held me back. It was time to pray and move my feet, as my spiritual counselor states. I was told by God in this dream, "Go for it!"

I look forward to more upcoming opportunities to share my story publicly to give people ideas of how I have learned to move past my own hurt, trauma and health issues. I believe we are all given an opportunity to learn from our mistakes, but I also believe it is important to share with others some of the tools that have helped you, as we are called to be servants, and I believe my purpose that God has given me here on this earth is to share my story, be vulnerable, and reach out to others who have also endured losing their parents, a spouse, unexplained health issues, and childhood abuse. Life is not easy, but there is a solution to have joy. For me, my joy has come from my loving father, and the acceptance in my heart of Jesus Christ who is the provider of the utmost peace and happiness.

# FIFTEEN

# Living With Peace

Seeking security with people is dumb. We need to seek security with God, first and foremost. Rely on God. I believe we can help others by helping them identify how to find the utmost peace and happiness after enduring trauma. We all have one heart, and we need to take the time to look within and find the message and purpose for each one of our lives.

I find peace in spending time with my girlfriends, practicing meditation and yoga, getting massages, attending retreats, reading, lying in the sun, and just enjoying every day and waking up each day to acknowledge that no matter what, it is a beautiful day. I had made several wrong choices in the past with all of the marriages that I forced upon myself and the men that I married, but it was all for a purpose. I can now see the lessons on love that I learned and can appreciate where I am today after enduring all of the hurt that I experienced, in addition to the hurt that I caused the men I had married. I have forgiven myself and give myself grace, and pray the men will also forgive me for the hurt that I caused them.

My first husband and I met shortly after my father died of a heart attack when I was eighteen years old. I was not ready to be married, and treated him poorly. He was a kind, sweet, athletic man that truly loved me. I threw him aside and hurt him deeply.

My second husband was the father of my two children and I chose to marry him after one month of knowing him. I was blessed with two beautiful boys and had some good times and a beautiful home, RV, toys, and the opportunity to stay with my children for three years. It is so important to truly know the character and values of your partner before marrying and having children. It broke my heart to break up my family and live separately, but it was the right decision for me at the time, as the relationship was not fulfilling and had become toxic for me.

My third husband was the love of my life, Biff Johnson. We were introduced by a mutual friend and had a love affair for two and a half years. Biff proposed to me and committed to being my life partner and was the most unselfish caretaker and lover to me. We married on November 6, 2010, and he died of a heart attack on March 24, 2011. This was my rock bottom.

My fourth husband was a rebound from Biff. We met at an outdoor concert venue (aka bar) and started our relationship with me still comparing all men to Biff. I was not ready to marry again and I was seeking another man to love my children. I pushed for this relationship and it was not right for me. We built this "dream home" that I thought would be my "white picket fence". I left him after two years and came home to California. I hurt this man.

I believe all the relationship choices and loss of loved ones has gotten me to where I am today, a woman of faith, with the ability to keep loving and remaining vulnerable, understanding, having strength, and finding peace and happiness in everyday life as God's test pilot here in Earth School.

It is key to become grounded and clear our energy to manifest what we want without chaos in our lives. For me, the chaos has not necessarily been self-driven, but until I can clear the energy, I will remain tired and unable to create a grounded, intimate relationship.

My children are souls that were created for me to guide, but I must release them to God.

I have found true strength in loss and trauma. I have discovered joy in my life. It has taken me many years to take a step back, remove myself from the wrong relationships, focus on who I really am, stop listening to false stories of who I am supposed to be as a manager in corporate America, or wife and mom living with white picket fence in my backyard.

I consider myself a woman with internal fortitude. I have kept going, stayed faithful, and remained positive contrary to my corporate experiences and health challenges, loss of loved ones, and difficulties in parenting.

I am a believer in prayer and meditation, but it takes practice and knowing how to meditate.

To have the ability to completely empty my mind of any thoughts and truly relax and go into the spiritual realm is a very challenging task for me. I believe that meditation needs to come from God. He created us with energy and energy chakras and we need to take that into consideration when meditating. I have had the blessed ability to see the white light move from the top of my head down to the bottom of my feet. I have felt that energy rush run throughout my body.

It is exhilarating that the "new age" meditation is based upon us humans being the ones in control and of most importance, which in all reality, God created meditation and energy in our bodies.

I enjoy the ability to be able to listen to scripture, soft music, and also work on the balances of my chakras to appreciate the body that God created for me to live in temporarily on this planet. It is so easy to get wrapped up in the flesh and what it can give us.

I have struggled with illness throughout my life and have had several auto-immune diseases. It helps me to envision a healthy, strong and natural body that has energy to balance me throughout life. I am at peace within my soul at this time of my life.

Our human bodies and all of creation in my opinion did not just "happen." It was a creation from our almighty God and our lives are a gift to give back to him and share the news of his son Jesus Christ being our savior from the sins that we have since the fall of Satan. He brings peace. (2 John 1:3) Let grace, mercy, and peace be with us in truth and love from God the Father and from Jesus.

# SIXTEEN

# Finding The Joy And Peace In Your Life

I am here to share with you, friends, that no matter what circumstances, what challenges we have in this lifetime, joy is the emotion evoked by well-being, success, or good fortune. Joy is caused by elation at the moment in time. We need to be focused on the here and now and look within for that exhilarating feeling when we know that there is a settled assurance that God is in control of all the details of our lives. We can have the confidence to know that ultimately, everything is going to be all right and the determined choice to praise God in every situation can be achieved.

I have shared with you throughout this book the tools that I use to experience joy within my soul include listening to worship music, practicing Holy Yoga, reading scripture and learning more about how Jesus loved others, and I also enjoy spending time in nature and witnessing the carefree wildlife. I love watching the waves at the ocean and the feeling that I have inside of me while walking on the beach. It brings me great joy to feel my toes in the sand, while listening to the crashing waves of the ocean.

I love driving up to the mountains and sitting between pine trees and listening to the wind whistle through the pines. When I lived in the desert I would hike up to the quiet areas where I heard the eagles and birds in the air. I would hear a lizard rustling through the bushes or watch cottontail hopping around the dirt roads with his carefree spirit.

It would give me pleasure watching the wildlife not experiencing the same anxiety that we struggle with here on earth as human beings. There is such an innocence in watching animals and how they are able to just exist without the concern of their future or dwelling on the past frustrations they may have experienced.

I studied trauma holy yoga and it gave me so much clarity. Our state of ourselves is so important. We are not fully responsible for what has happened to us in the past if it was something we could not control, but we can take the experience and learn from it, and train ourselves to change when we approach various circumstances. We do not have to be a product of our environment.

When we have a community of support, it changes how resilient we are. We have self-awareness, and we all have different emotional intelligence. Find the right community for you.

We have the responsibility to love others, but also to love ourselves. Our senses and our feelings can be triggered by past experiences if we were traumatized in the past. We can be skeptical of our senses. (Psalm 16:1–9) Reserve ourselves in God. We can put our body at peace and not be hijacked in traumatic experiences. We can endure the lack of feeling of safety in our own bodies from our past memories. God's presence will come into our own physical being. We can have an internal sense of safety. We need to understand that the true source of safety is from God. (Exodus 33:14) God said, My presence will go with you. I'll see the journey to the end.

It is a gift to wake up and breathe. We need to choose to allow God to align our days with peace, joy and awakenings.

God uses our suffering as a way of transforming us from survival mode to thriving. Grounding and breathing techniques in Holy Yoga have taught me to set aside the past, to not focus on the feelings of shame, guilt, unhappiness, and look within and focus on the heart chakra where God places his utmost joy.

Jesus Christ has given me this capacity to trust him in knowing I can trust, feel happy from the inside, and remain in that exhilarating feeling of true happiness, acceptance, and joy within my body. Our Earth School experience can be joyful.

If we come to Christ as a child, it gives us the ability to look at our existence from an innocent standpoint and have the resilience that a small child has during its time of curiosity, learning, accepting, and truly letting themselves take risks and believe that it will all be okay. Dr. Carolyn Leaf states in her book, *Cleaning up Mental Mess,* "Your mind can be renewed, your value was established in childhood, we are made to decide about our own value." Similarly, (Matthew 18:3) tells us, "Unless we come like little children, we will not enter heaven." This verse is so profound to me. We need to stay vulnerable, accepting, and open to what is available to us in this lifetime. Our job here in Earth School is to serve, give, learn, and trust.

I enjoy listening to Wayne Dyer and his teachings. Dr Dyer states in his book, *Change Your Thoughts, Change Your Life: Living the Wisdom of the Tao,* that 99 percent of who we are, we can't touch, see, or smell. Our conscious awareness is what really matters.

We need to love ourselves, be gentle and nicer to ourselves. This is considered Christ consciousness. For me, when I am practicing Holy Yoga, I wrap my arms around myself and give myself a hug and envision myself loving my own body. When we have a successful faith life, it starts with us learning to love ourselves. We are not to worship ourselves or be narcisstic. God wants us to go through our lives filled with love towards others and ourselves. If we choose to love ourselves first, it gives us the capability to love others. We are created as human beings to share love to others, and to ourselves. We can give this love and show others the joy that lies within us and try to explain to others what it feels like to truly live with joy inside of us. What comes out of us is always what is inside of us. If we choose to focus on the good things, the beauty in our surroundings, the positive aspects of the people that we encounter, it can make such a difference in the outlook we have each day when we wake up knowing there are lessons to be learned and they can be positive. We need to accept each day as a gift and opportunity to give back, help others, and learn from our mistakes and move forward.

We can look at each circumstance daily and instead of getting angry if it does not go our way, realize it is all part of the lesson for the day to teach ourselves to not take other people's reactions personally.

We all have our own story and capabilities of dealing with our own trauma and challenges. We can only focus on our own way of handling our reactions. It is not our responsibility to change other people. We were put on this earth to be an example. It is not for us to judge guilt or shame others into thinking they are wrong, unaccepted, or should be ashamed of their own actions.

We do not know where we are going, unless we know where we are. This is directly from Genesis 1.

The brokenness in the garden is the same that is cutting in on us now. Shame immediately comes into existence here in our Earth School experience. Self-conscious emotions such as shame and price are emotions that typically focus on the self of the person who feels them. In the garden of eden, Eve disobeyed God's direction to not eat of the apple that was forbidden to eat, and she and Adam immediately felt shame in their bodies once they disobeyed God. We are born into this sin of the feeling of shame.

When we experience trauma in our lives, it can exacerbate the feeling that we have of being shameful of our own body and feeling guilty about the bad choices that we make for our lives. God gives us the ability to ask for forgiveness and the security of knowing that He is in acceptance of us as human beings that are born into sin. We have the opportunity to receive forgiveness and accept our own bodies and decisions that we make as human beings. We will make mistakes, but we are forgiven if we choose to ask God for forgiveness. (Matthew

6:14-15) For if you forgive men their trespasses, your heavenly Father will also forgive you.

Confession gives us our authority back. (Romans 10:11-13). Scripture reassures us, No one who trusts God like this, heart and soul, will ever regret it. It's exactly the same no matter what a person's religious background may be; the same God for all of us, acting the same incredibly generous way to everyone who calls out for help. Everyone who calls, "Help, God!", gets help. When I am stating my mantra of, *We all have one heart* this is what I mean by we all are created equally as human flesh, with a human heart, no matter where we live, or what religious practice we choose. Jesus told us that if we believe in Him as the son of God, we are forgiven and can receive the gift of salvation.

For me, I choose to believe in the existence of Jesus as the son of God, and this has given me the comfort in knowing there is a life in eternity that is available to those who accept the gift of forgiveness. I can move past the shame from my own choices that I have made in this lifetime and be forgiven.

The opposite of shame, guilt, and fear is courage, joy, and love. We can move our emotional vibration to higher frequencies through meditation and visualization. This could give us the courage and ability to love others and have peace within us while walking on this earth.

As an example of God's love and positive energy, we can show others that there is a purpose to everyone's life and we need to use our time to focus on the positive aspects of life, no matter what circumstances we are enduring. If it's not good, it's not over! For example, if we are in traffic, we can work on ourselves during this time in the car to control our anxiety, anger, and aggressive feelings towards the negative aspect of this current experience.

I choose to play positive YouTube podcasts and listen to various motivational speakers. I have enjoyed some of Oprah's *Super Soul Sundays*, and any other beneficial talks I can find in order to stay focused on the positive, knowing I cannot control traffic.

I have studied Holy Yoga and listened to various teachings and podcasts to help me learn more about how I can heal from past trauma. Brooke Boone wrote the book *Holy Yoga,* and I had the pleasure of being involved in an organization called *Arras Sisters*, where I met with Brooke in person and heard her testimony of how she moved past her own hurt and trauma and created the practice of Holy Yoga.

*Arras Sisters* is an organization that empowers women to share their story and reach out to others to help them by communicating their own stories and how they came past hurt and found joy. I worked with *Arras Sisters* to prepare my speaker reel to share my own story and make it public. You can find my reel on my website. www. serenaestes.com

We all have a soul and a mind, as well as our emotional and physical state of being. We can focus on the serenity of prayer in knowing that we cannot control others or our circumstances and we need to identify what we can control and understand the difference. We can choose to accept, have serenity and move past the guilt, shame and negative connotation of any circumstance we have here in Earth School.

Our experiences are aligned with our vibration. Other people can feel our energy. We must have gratitude for our growth and the layers.

Our self-worth is identified by the work that we do within ourselves in challenging our own decisions and how we treat ourselves in the process of enduring trials.

There is disruptive energy on this planet.

We can find peace on the path. We can heal ourselves if we believe and have faith in knowing that if we trust God, it will all be okay.

I have struggled with fears of financial security my whole life. It stems from the anxiety that I had as a child of the uncertainty of what would happen next.

"Pray, and move your feet," is a mantra that my spiritual guide Dana has taught me. I have always been driven, but this particular mantra has kept me focused on what I am praying for.

The healing that has taken place for me has happened through using tools like taking deep breaths, meditating, staying in Scripture, and spending time alone in reflecting on what God's plan is for my life. It gives me the chance to take a look at the lessons and what I have learned from all of them.

As I have shared previously, I love spending time in the mountains. Specifically Big Bear, California. I have spent time in Big Bear since 1976; it's a very special place in my heart. My father sold real estate in the desert and he would come up here in the 1970s after his diagnosis with cancer, living in the high desert, trying to get out of the rat race of the Hollywood lifestyle and getting out of the madness of the fast-paced life.

We can find the Holy Spirit wherever we look for him. He is always willing to reveal himself. He never leaves or forsakes us. I love life in the mountains and desert; it soothes my soul knowing God is in control of our atmosphere.

I love the trees, serenity, peace, authenticity, and the good atmosphere in the Southern and Northern Californian mountains. The experience of going to the mountains gives me the ability to appreciate the air, as it's cleaner than in the city. I like the feeling I get being around authentic people living in a small town and surrounding myself with honest, hard working people. It is cleansing for my soul. There is nothing like the feeling of the peace of the mountain air and wildlife of the mountains. God is good!

Our Lord reveals himself in nature. I feel so blessed to have the capability to breathe, stay still, and know God is in control of our destiny. God will show us the way. The main thing is, we need to find peace and balance.

During the coronavirus times, it gave us the perspective of what really matters. Breathe!! I find it interesting that God had allowed this virus to attack the breath, in knowing that our Lord is in control of our breath. Without breath, there is no life. We take that fact for granted.

I have a tendency to live ahead of my time, focusing on where I want to be instead of where I am today. In prayer each day, I choose to breathe in thankfulness and not allow the past pain to control my feelings. This all comes back to faith. When God says it will happen, our only answer should be, "Ok, make it happen!"

We need to be in a loving, compassionate space at both work and at home. We must look at life from an observation lens, not from frustration. We need to breathe, and let it go. An example of being a more loving person and compassionate towards others could be learning how to accept our children as a gift from God that were created with their own path and story. It has been difficult for me to not want to control my children's destiny and make choices for them. I tend to want to do the work for them and not surrender it to God to allow them to experience their own trauma and challenges. As a mom, I have wanted them to not have to experience the pain that I have in my life.

In the work environment, I believe it is important to start each day reading scripture in knowing that we will possibly have difficulty in communication and potentially have a challenging task to complete. If we start our day with the Lord, praying for guidance and direction to have the right responses and reactions when we are presented with our challenges, it makes a difference during the course of the day dealing with difficult people and circumstances. An example of how to do this is to use the daily YouVersion Bible App where you can select various plans. For me, I have used this bible app each day reading the verse of the day and selecting various topics for plans. This app has plans on patience, faith over fear, love, anxiety, marriage, dating and work.

# THE FINAL SYNOPSIS
# OF CREATING THE
# WHITE PICKET FENCE

My mantra is, "We all have one heart, a purpose and a story."

In all of our lessons in life, we make good choices and bad, but with God on our side giving us the right direction (if we choose to listen), we can understand the reason for our circumstances, challenges, and the choices we make.

> I own the mistakes I have made. I choose to learn from them and have spent the past five years learning to stop, listen, and discern what is best. I have made mistakes in my career, relationships, and endured many health challenges. I have the courage to move apart from the hurt, trauma and live in the moment by using the tools that I have learned to help myself not to continue to live in self destruction.

## COURAGE

The hardest part of stepping out in courage is giving up the control we can believe we actually have. I have trusted in corporate America, climbing the ladder, achieving a false sense of security with monetary compensation. The only true way to have acceptance is to release the

147

control that we think we have to God. We must have the courage to do the work in learning tools that help us to not make destructive choices for our life.

Many women (and men) choose to live in this physode that there is a "white picket fence" livelihood out there for us. As I had explained earlier in my definition of the white picket fence, we tend to make the wrong decisions for our life to look good and feel good by making the wrong choices for intimate partners for our lives. I had this physode that I had to get married early, birth children and live in an expensive home, obtain a college education and obtain a certain income in order to be accepted by society.

What we may not take into consideration is that we must choose to seek advice from the right sources, listen to the truth that we are being shown, and stop ourselves from continuing along the same paths of destruction.

After over fifty years of self-destruction, over 14 surgeries, 4 marriages, and enduring witnessing your children with their own struggles trying to grow up, I can now say that I can truly look within myself, love myself, listen to God speaking truth to me, and not live in a fear-based consciousness mindset.

We can be whole, live in peace, and find the joy that lives inside of us. For me, that is incorporating the love of Jesus Christ, the Holy Spirit, and welcoming him into my body, my soul, and my spirit. I have found the ministry and practice of Holy Yoga on a daily basis, along with meditating on the Scripture in the Bible, helps me learn how to stop making the wrong decisions for my life and letting the wrong people reside with me and influence me away from loving myself, first and foremost, and focusing on my purpose of sharing my story and breathing peace into my life.

I host Holy Yoga retreats with my tribe and welcome you to join us each quarter. Please visit my website, http://www.serenaestes.com

Find your purpose, friends; we all have one. I welcome the challenge of this Earth School and the lessons that I will continue to learn.

Life has not been easy, but I am in a great place and have the desire to share how I have now become a whole person, not relying upon an intimate relationship, but finding my peace with my true husband, Jesus Christ, who will never forsake me or leave me, and will always remain steadfast in his love for me.

Faithfulness breeds integrity. Never stop talking to God and stay focused relentlessly praying for your contentment, peace and good health. We all pray to the same God.

Evidence of God's blessing isn't always monetary compensation, but it's always contentment.

We all have a purpose, friends. I encourage you to find yours.

A woman with a heart of thankfulness and a desire to honor God leads to others coming to know God and honor Him as well. - Pastor Jim Jackson, Orchard Church, Temecula, CA

# ABOUT THE AUTHOR

Serena Estes was born and raised in Southern California. She is the mother of two boys, and has endured the loss of both of her parents at a young age, many health issues, and lost the love of her life suddenly after five and a half months of marriage.

Serena posts daily inspirations on Instagram at One Heart at: serena estes.one heart and has the desire to share her story and how she found peace and understanding; how to stop searching for the "white picket fence" after making many wrong choices in relationships, friendships, and family issues.

Serena is a Holy Yoga instructor and hosts quarterly retreats to share her story of how she found peace and an understanding of the purpose of her life. Serena is also a public motivational speaker, and has taken the "gifts" of the life lessons learned here in Earth School to help others who have also suffered the loss of loved ones.

Serena is a woman with tremendous faith, and attributes her healing to her true Healer, Jesus Christ. She is not a religious person, but honors the Holy Bible as the ultimate answer for how she has healed through many tragedies, losses, and health issues.

Serena has learned how to look within herself instead of to others to fulfill her destiny and purpose. She has learned how to be by herself and enjoy it. She encourages others to seek the Lord for all counsel and not people for the answers.

Serena has been blessed with wonderful friends in her life, but has struggled with a weakness of seeking advice from others instead of our good Lord. He is the only one with the true answers. She is now preparing workshops for specific steps on how to learn to use the tools that she has learned and help others who have also suffered from trauma, health issues, and loss, in addition to making the wrong decisions in life by creating this "white picket fence" syndrome that many people create to have the "perfect life" in believing material possessions and seeking a partner in life that might not be God's choice.

Serena has learned to fall in love with herself instead of creating the story of the perfect intimate relationship and continuing to marry the wrong partners that were not right for her. She is now in a healthy place with having the ability to accept that she has made mistakes and forgive herself.

# ENCOURAGING WORDS FROM FRIENDS OF SERENA

The day I met Serena I knew she would be my friend for life. She has a fierce spirit and honesty that my daughters and I connected to immediately. I have seen her experience loss so deep it would cripple someone else. I have seen her battle health issues and battle the addiction of a very close loved one. But through it all her strong faith has carried her through. She sets an example for me and others to follow each and every day. ~ **Lisa Nugent, Cedar Park, Texas**

When I met Serena for the first time, her heart was shattered after suffering the loss of her husband, Biff. Over the years, I've witnessed her encounter numerous other personal challenges. What inspires me the most about Serena is that she is unwavering in her faith, belief, and devotion to her walk with God. It doesn't matter what comes her way, she remains true to herself and her process of healing. While her story is powerful, it's her strength and conviction that "all things work for the good for those who believe in Him" that is deeply inspiring." ~ **Jayne Clark, Jayne Clark Coaching**

I have had the pleasure of having Serena in my life for over 20yrs. I have witnessed many of life's happy moments, challenging moments and sad moments. In all of these years I have never seen Serena's faith waiver, not once! Even during the most difficult times, she leans more into her faith to get through it! Faith is at her core! So let's look at the word F A I T H and how Serena lives it every day:

- **F = Friends** – Serena has a huge tribe of friends who care for her and she cares for them deeply. These friends are her foundation that helps to move her forward in life!
- **A = Attitude**- A positive attitude will get you far in life! Serena now sees the direct impact that having a positive attitude can bring especially in her journey with the Holy Yoga Retreats.
- **I = Integrity**- Such an important attribute. This represents who you are, your character: trustworthiness and honesty. Life has challenged Serena's integrity and each time she has held firm and held her ground.
- **T = Truth**- This is a powerful word! One has to stay true to themselves and to their beliefs. One of the challenges we have is to accept the truth, even when we don't want to hear it. Truth can be difficult to accept and to give but it keeps one on the right path in life! Serena walks and talks the truth!
- **H = Holy Spirit**- recently thanks in part to Holy Yoga, Serena has come to know the power and joy that the Holy Spirit can bring. One of the most powerful gifts we have is the Holy Spirit to help guide us through life's challenges.

FAITH has gotten Serena through life! I can't imagine her life without FAITH. My prayer for Serena; continue to understand your faith, continue to talk about your faith and continue to practice our faith.

May God Bless you as you share your story
~**Claire Weiland, Huntington Beach, CA**

I have known Serena Estes for over 5 years. Our hearts were knitted together instantly. If I had one word that describes her best it would be "servant". I have seen her in action with children, teenagers and adults. She is a wonderful storyteller and she always speaks from her heart.

Whether it be ministry or speaking on stage, Serena has a way of pulling you in with her compassion and desire to convey truth. --Kimberley Loska, As a Heart Speaks

Serena can be reached at the following website and social media:

- www.serenaestes.com
- oneheartserenaestes@gmail.com
- Instagram: https://www.instagram.com/serenaestes.oneheart
- Facebook: https://m.facebook.com/pg/SerenaEstes.OneHeart

Serena's "Mantra"

## WE ALL HAVE ONE HEART, A STORY AND A PURPOSE